THE TWELFTH-CENTURY RENAISSANCE

THE
TWELFTH-CENTURY
RENAISSANCE

Edited by CHARLES R. YOUNG

Duke University

HOLT, RINEHART AND WINSTON
New York · Chicago · San Francisco · Atlanta
Dallas · Montreal · Toronto · London · Sydney

Cover illustration: Sculpture from the central portal on the west façade of Chartres Cathedral, called the Royal Portal (1145–1150), which comprises a portion of an archivolt symbolizing the liberal arts. (*Left*) Pythagoras, reputed founder of music theory, is shown writing in medieval fashion with a desk over his knees. On the wall behind him is a shelf holding a supply of pens and sponges for erasures. (*Right*) Grammar, symbolized by a teacher, holds an open book in one hand and the disciplinary switch in the other over the heads of two young pupils, one of whom is laughing and pulling the other's hair. (*Houvet, Chartres*)

Copyright © 1969 by Holt, Rinehart and Winston, Inc.
All Rights Reserved
Library of Congress Catalog Card Number: 77-89843
SBN: 03-079805-1
Printed in the United States of America
9 8 7 6 5 4 3 2 1

CONTENTS

Sculpture from the central portal on the west façade of Chartres Cathedral (1145–1150). Music holds a psaltery on her lap and strikes a set of three chime bells, an allusion to the Pythagorean discovery of the mathematical ratios of the perfect intervals—the octave, the fifth, and the fourth. To the left is a monochord, used to calculate the intervals and for accuracy of pitch, and hanging below the bell is a viol. (*Houvet, Chartres*)

INTRODUCTION

In the modern world the term renaissance has been commonly used to describe any unusual burst of cultural activity, but this has not always been its meaning, for in its origins the term had a more specific sense. In the fourteenth and fifteenth centuries the Italian humanists, reacting vigorously against the immediate past, began to reject the heritage of the centuries that separated them from the glories of ancient Rome, and it was in this context that the idea of "the Middle Ages" arose, of a period of cultural darkness from which these humanists were struggling to emerge. Increasingly these men viewed their own age as a dawn of a new era, one in which the rebirth of classical culture was taking place. In the mid-nineteenth century, moreover, these views received seeming scholarly approval when Jules Michelet, soon joined by Jacob Burckhardt, adopted the term renaissance to differentiate this new period of classically oriented humanistic activity from the Middle Ages, which continued to be seen as a millennium of cultural darkness.

Nevertheless, toward the end of the nineteenth century historians began to discover that at least some medieval artists and writers had known and used the works of classical antiquity, thus forcing a revision of their estimate of medieval culture. By using the concept of renaissance to describe their discoveries, they forcefully challenged the then widely held view that the medieval centuries had been nothing more than "the Dark Ages." A landmark in medieval studies followed in 1927 with the publication of Charles Homer Haskins' *The Renaissance of the Twelfth Century*, a masterly synthesis which crystallized earlier discoveries and popularized the idea that the intellectual developments of the twelfth century, based on the classics as they were, were fully worthy of being deemed a renaissance. Rarely has a reviewer's judgment been so clearly justified as the one that predicted that Haskins' book would become the standard interpretation of the period. Thus, although a few scholars have recently questioned the appropriateness of his renaissance terminology, most have been content to concentrate either on particular aspects of twelfth-century cultural revival or on the problem of the relationship between it and other periods of Western civilization.

Haskins places the origins of his renaissance before 1100 and holds that it ended about 1250, when it was replaced by the scholasticism of the later thirteenth century. In so doing, he emphasizes only cultural trends, omitting

1

all mention of the other changes and developments that characterized the age. This emphasis contrasts markedly with that of Dana Carleton Munro, whose views appear in the first selection. Today, the chief value of Munro's early article is that it shows the very general terms in which the twelfth-century renaissance was being discussed prior to Haskins' synthesis, and although most scholars have chosen to follow Haskins in confining their research to cultural developments, differences in interpretive scope still remain. In some ways Friedrich Heer's approach represents a return to Munro's broad interpretation, but his discussion, unlike Munro's, is controlled by a conception of the twelfth century as an "open society"; cultural developments are discussed only within this larger framework and are used largely to provide evidence for that "openness" which Heer sees as the leading characteristic of the period.

A fundamentally different technique is employed by Richard W. Southern who relates social and cultural developments by always studying the individual and his cultural contributions within the context of the world in which he lived. In discussing Peter of Blois, for example, Southern does not limit his remarks to the significance of Peter's correspondence; rather, he brings in the practical aspects of Peter's career as well as those trends in twelfth-century society that made his writings popular. As a result, society and culture become so inextricably interlinked that neither, in Southern's view, can be understood without reference to the other.

In short, while the opening selections all point to the twelfth century as a period of change and intellectual ferment, each differs in its approach and emphasis. The reader's problem is to weigh the contribution of each, selecting from their varied details those elements that seem to contribute most to an understanding of the twelfth century and of its principal trends.

Another aspect of the problem is the very ambiguity of the term renaissance, particularly when applied to the twelfth century. Some scholars using it insist that it refers only to the rebirth of strictly classical culture, but others employ it more loosely to mean any general revival of learning. Nevertheless, even though differences of this type continue to complicate scholarly discussions, research interest has increasingly tended to shift away from such terminological questions as whether the degree of classical influence in the twelfth century warrants the term renaissance toward an investigation of the true nature of cultural movements. Thus, for example, the question has been raised whether this period was merely a stage in a continuous humanistic tradition which stretched from ancient Rome to the Italian Renaissance, or whether it was a period so distinctive in its individual characteristics that it should more properly be seen as a separate cultural era understandable only on its own terms without reference to other times. Certainly the twelfth century exhibited an interest in literary studies, in the "humane letters" of the ancients, that might be termed humanistic in the strict sense, but what was the relation between this trend in the twelfth century and scholasticism in the thirteenth—let alone Italian humanism in the fourteenth? Various answers have been given to these questions, some in the selections that follow, and all of them may be taken as illustrative of how historical interpretations are developed and tested in the crucible of scholarly debate.

Jean Leclercq is among the scholars who stress continuity between the culture of antiquity and that of the twelfth century. His individual contribution lies in his depiction of monastic culture as the vigorous product of the liturgical life of the monasteries, an interpretation sharply at variance with the traditional one of monks passively copying manuscripts. While his argument may explain literary studies in monastic centers, it was never meant to deal with the whole scope of the twelfth-century renaissance. Indeed, Leclercq's larger thesis is that in the twelfth century there was a monastic culture distinct from the intellectual movements that arose outside the monastic walls. Whether the literary and artistic influences of antiquity were strong enough beyond the monastery to indicate that twelfth-century culture formed part of a continuous humanistic tradition linking Rome and Renaissance Italy is a question that Leclercq leaves to other scholars.

And here there are many difficulties. For one thing, both artists and historians in the twelfth century lacked any feeling of historical perspective, of the distance between their own times and antiquity. Because of this failing, both Eva Matthews Sanford, who specialized in historical writing, and William S. Heckscher, who was concerned primarily with art and architecture, were led to reject the concept of renaissance as being inappropriate for the twelfth century, for they both felt that renaissance, with its meaning of rebirth, hardly fitted artists and writers so seemingly unaware either that antiquity had ended centuries before or that it had been "reborn" in their own time. To men of the twelfth century, they argued, such humanism as existed would have appeared not a rebirth but rather part of the general development of thought that connected antiquity with the age in which they lived.

Yet, consciously or not, the artistic themes of antiquity were usually revived and transformed by those who employed them in the twelfth century. Both Sanford and Heckscher recognize this fact in their studies. As a result, however, the possibility arises that the culture which emerged in the twelfth century, a culture greatly changed from that of antiquity and endowed with a unity and distinctive characteristics of its own, should be better considered as a new and different movement in cultural history. Hans Liebeschütz tends to this view in his thorough work on John of Salisbury, for although he finds precedents for John's Christian humanism in the Church Fathers, notably in the blend of classicism and Christianity embodied in the thought of St. Jerome, he nevertheless feels that the Christian humanism of the twelfth century, while not unique, is genuinely a distinct development within medieval culture, not simply a prolongation of the pagan humanism of ancient Rome to which it was unconnected by any direct line of descent. These qualifications, while not entirely contrary to the views of Haskins, are still enough in opposition to suggest that Haskins' views ought to be modified.

The relationship of the twelfth-century renaissance to scholasticism is another subject on which scholars have taken opposing views. As a historian of philosophy, Étienne Gilson has eloquently stated the case for including his field (and, consequently, all of scholasticism) within the bounds of humanism. In his interpretation the thought of St. Thomas Aquinas becomes the acme of medieval humanism, while the thirteenth century becomes the period in which trends begun in the twelfth finally came to fruition. A similar conclusion is reached by Gérard Paré, Adrien Brunet, and Pierre Tremblay in their study of medieval education, for even though they see a marked change in the thirteenth century away from literary studies toward law, philosophy, and theology, this change can still be viewed as the natural culmination of the twelfth-century renaissance so long as no special emphasis is placed on continuity of literary form.

Gilson's interpretation has been particularly attractive to certain Catholic scholars, but others like Dom David Knowles have denied the perpetuation of humanistic ideals by the scholastics. Indeed, it is hard to see that there are any clear divisions of opinion along sectarian lines. Knowles acknowledges the dependence of the scholastics upon ancient philosophers and the scholastic reverence for the past, but at the same time he emphasizes, in opposition to Gilson, that the scholastics adapted the thought of the ancients to serve the new philosophic purposes of a wholly different world view. Moreover, no such coupling of centuries and intellectual movements is possible for the scholar like Knowles whose primary concern is literary. As Joseph de Ghellinck, a Jesuit, points out, the abandonment of grammatical and literary studies for philosophy and theology brought to an end a whole variety of interests that had flourished in the twelfth century. In his view, medieval humanism fell victim to the dual onslaught of Aristotelian logic and a utilitarian emphasis in the few literary studies that continued.

Whatever the reader may conclude about the relationship between the twelfth and thirteenth centuries, it is perfectly clear that the literary humanism of the earlier period has certain similarities to that of the Italian Renaissance. The final selections are directed toward answering the question whether these similarities point to direct influence from the earlier movement to the later. In other words, was the literary humanism of the twelfth century essentially an independent cultural movement complete in itself, or was it the somewhat remote ancestor of the Italian Renaissance? William A. Nitze uses the contrast between the absence in the twelfth century of any self-conscious awareness and its decided presence in the Italian Renaissance to argue that the intellectual outlook of the earlier period was fundamentally different from that of the fifteenth century, which emphasized both the separation from antiquity and the necessity for a rebirth of classical culture. He further holds that to identify the dominant trend of one period with that of another only leads to confusion in our understanding of either.

The opposite point of view is represented by Paul Renucci whose thesis stresses the continuity of the humanistic tradition from the medieval to the Renaissance period. Not only was the twelfth century a period of true humanism, it also prepared the way for the humanism of the Italian Renaissance. In this framework the rationalism of the thirteenth-century scholastics becomes the connecting link between two similar periods whose only essential difference was one of direction. According to Renucci, Dante was the first step in this new direction, so important for all of European thought, and the medieval assumptions influencing Dante can no more be separated from the new views that came from him than he himself can be split into two separate individuals.

By now it should be apparent that the study of twelfth-century culture developed in reaction to the oversimplified and antimedieval views expressed by most Renaissance scholars in the later nineteenth century. Even the title of Haskins' *The Renaissance of the Twelfth Century* seems to have been chosen as a deliberate challenge to these interpretations, and subsequent research has indeed demonstrated the vitality, richness, and variety of medieval culture, particularly in the twelfth century. Many of the differences among scholars have arisen from their failure adequately to recognize this richness and variety in formulating their views of medieval cultural activity and its relation to other periods in Western civilization. Other differences have grown from the tendency to employ ambiguous terminology. Thus, for example, the process of discussing medieval cultural developments in terms of renaissances has caused unnecessary confusion simply because some people have defined the term rigorously while others have found renaissances wherever there was any interest in classical culture, no matter how muted or distorted. It is probably too late to abandon the concept of a twelfth-century renaissance, but one can hope that our understanding of the Middle Ages has progressed to the point where the term can be treated as little more than a conventional rubric.

Perhaps the solution to these difficulties is offered by Paul Oskar Kristeller in his plea for historical pluralism. The problem is to construct an interpretation in which the dominant trends of every period—the trends that link one epoch with another—stand out, and yet an interpretation in which the individual richness and variety of each period is in no way neglected. Vague comparisons of Italy in the fourteenth century with France in the twelfth have little value; only more rigorous methods of analysis give promise of placing the continuing scholarly debate on firmer footing, and it is for this reason that recent work on the twelfth century has tended to be technical in nature.

Whether complete scholarly agreement is ever reached, it is clear that the study of the twelfth-century renaissance has been one avenue by which a more accurate and, in a sense, more favorable assessment of the Middle Ages has been achieved. Since Haskins first made this problem one of general concern, attempts to put the high periods of medieval culture into proper perspective have led to a better understanding not only of medieval culture itself, but also of its relation to antiquity and to the modern world, whose debt to the Middle Ages is only now beginning to be appreciated.

In the reprinted selections footnotes appearing in the original sources have in general been omitted unless they contribute to the argument or better understanding of the selection.

DANA CARLETON MUNRO (1866–1933) taught medieval history at the universities of Pennsylvania, Wisconsin, and Princeton. His special interest was the Crusades, a subject on which he published articles and wrote a book, *The Kingdom of the Crusaders* (published posthumously in 1935), preparatory to a comprehensive history he planned but never lived to write. Graduates of his seminar figure prominently among the scholars who have produced three volumes of the multivolume history of the Crusades now being published under the aegis of the Mediaeval Academy of America. His influence as a teacher was given wider scope by his successful textbook, *The Middle Ages* (1921). When the American Historical Association in 1906 devoted a session to the twelfth-century renaissance, Munro delivered the principal paper, a synthesis of scholarly opinion on the subject in the broad terms being used at that time for the discussion of the twelfth century. To Munro, the spirit of independence, along with a new interest in science and an emphasis on the application of learning, were the characteristics of the twelfth century that made it a period of new life.*

A Period of New Life

Renaissance is popularly understood to mean the revival of classical arts and literature. Taken in this narrow sense, the expression, "Renaissance of the twelfth century," is misleading. It is true that during this century, in John of Salisbury,[1] the cultivation of the Latin literature reached the highest point attained during the Middle Ages. It is also true that other authors of this period were steeped in the beauty of the Latin writings, and, after the model of their masters, wrote prose and verse which are not without merit. Some of their productions have even been attributed to classical authors. The poems of Archbishop Baldric of Dol are written in the style of Virgil or of Ovid. William of Tyre[2] puts

[1] His major work, the *Policraticus*, is filled with quotations from his wide reading in classical literature. In the *Metalogicon* he described the methods of teaching literature that dominated the cathedral school of Chartres when he was a student.—Ed.

[2] William of Tyre (*ca.* 1130–1186) wrote a history of Palestine valuable for the first crusade and the early years of the twelfth century.—Ed.

* Dana Carleton Munro, "The Renaissance of the Twelfth Century," *Annual Report of the American Historical Association for the Year 1906* (Washington, 1908), vol. I, pp. 45–49.

into the mouths of his characters speeches which are clearly composed under the influences of Livy and other Roman historians. But this was in reality a culmination of the work of the preceding generations, and not a renaissance. Furthermore, even when this delight in classical literature was at its height some were decrying the devotion to nonpractical studies. John of Salisbury has much to say of the Cornificians, the opponents of the classics. His arguments are weighty and remind us of those used at the present day. But he was fighting a losing battle, and classical studies were destined to suffer an eclipse from which they would emerge only in the days of the Italian renaissance.

The term "Renaissance of the twelfth century" may be justified if renaissance be taken in its true meaning of new life, for the twelfth century was a period of wonderful advance along very many different lines. It has become commonplace to speak of the modernity of Abelard's point of view.[3] But only gradually has it been realized how completely he was in this an exponent of the new ideas of his age. This delay has been due mainly to the fact that attention has been concentrated, to a great degree, on the political and constitutional history, on the dramatic struggles between church and state, on the great crusading expeditions, or in the domain of thought on the development of scholasticism. Too often have we forgotten that we still delight in and imitate the most characteristic productions of the age, the literature of chivalry, and the Gothic architecture. As soon as we turn our attention to these we realize how rapid the evolution had been. . . .

[3] This interpretation of Abelard's rationalism as foreshadowing modern attitudes is no longer considered valid.—Ed.

The most marked characteristic of the twelfth century was the evolution of the spirit of independence. This was manifest in many different modes of thought and action. Above all, men became less subservient to authority. They began to doubt whether what they had been taught was entirely true. The discussions during the investiture struggle[4] had been somewhat influential in shaking their faith, because the partisans had set up one tradition against another and had denied the validity of tradition opposed to their own point of view. Again, absolute trust was weakened when men found that some statements which had been accepted without question were not true. The crusaders sometimes made naive confessions that they had not found the conditions in the Holy Land such as they had been taught to expect. The evil lives of some members of the clergy aroused the suspicion that such men might not be fit to administer the sacraments. This doubt, by no means new, led to heresy. As a whole this weakening of trust in what had been accepted would not cause an entire rejection of all authority, but rather a shifting from one authority to another. The twelfth century has been called "The age of Aristotle," because his writings were revered and furnished the method and some of the subject-matter for the thought of the age.

The shifting of authority was due in part to the fact that the influence and wealth of the nobility and clergy had decreased and the inhabitants of cities had been advancing in importance and in self-consciousness. The twelfth cen-

[4] The investiture struggle (1075–1122) produced a large number of writings and stimulated the development of political theories both in support of the spiritual authority of the popes and in justification of the secular authority of the emperors.—Ed.

tury was an age of great democratic opportunity. Individuals like Suger[5] rose from the peasant class to high rank and great wealth. Guilds of workmen obtained their enfranchisement and governed themselves by regulations which they themselves made. Communes obtained charters and became influential by the wealth of their citizens. The latter were very proud of their independence and inclined to carry their freedom into the domain of religious thought. The Church had, as a rule, been hostile to the establishment of the communes. Also, its attention was not directed in the twelfth century to reaching the people by its sermons or teaching. With the exception of the preaching of the crusades, the sermons were not of a character to interest and to hold the attention of the people. Consequently they listened willingly to the preaching of heretics and lost much of their former feeling of devotion to the Church. The divisions between the classes of society were partially effaced by the decline of the upper classes and the rise of the lower. The courtly literature of the twelfth century shows the envy of the nobles for the citizens, but also their admiration of the wealthy and populous cities. On the other hand, the bourgeois literature, the fabliaux[6] and the songs of the Goliards,[7] show a mocking contempt for clergy and nobility. The latter

also illustrates the irreverence which was fast becoming one of the characteristics of society as a whole. This spared no one and no subject. God and the devil, Aristotle and the Pope, Canon and feudal law, Cistercians and priests were held up to ridicule.

The literature, as a whole, shows similar changes in the spirit of the age. At the beginning of the century the vernacular literature is represented by religious poems inculcating the virtues of asceticism and humility, or by chansons lauding piety to God and fidelity to the feudal lord. In the epopée [epic poetry], love of woman becomes a dominant theme and the joys of life are described; fighting, rich banquets, and luxurious garments are dwelt upon to satiety. Later come such fabliaux as the villain who achieves paradise by pleading, or the jongleur who shakes dice with St. Peter. At the end of the century all of these types existed side by side.

Again, hasty generalization would lead to serious error. These citizens who were so intent upon making money and so irreverent in their attitude were capable of deep and long-continued devotion. This is the period when the great cathedrals were built, when the citizens contributed their property year after year for the erection of a building which should satisfy their religious aspirations and beautify their city. They gave their labor, too. Far from home, the inhabitants of Chartres might be seen, men, women, and children, yoked to the heavy carts which bore the building materials. Day after day their weary march continued, and when they stopped for the night nothing was to be heard but confession and prayer.

A second great characteristic of the age was the devotion to science. It is significant that even at Chartres, which was

---

[5] Suger (*ca.* 1801–1151), abbot of St. Denis, was chief minister of King Louis VI of France. His book describing the rebuilding of the church of St. Denis is one of the best contemporary accounts of the beginnings of Gothic architecture.—Ed.

[6] Fabliaux were popular stories whose point was often to make the clergy or nobility appear ridiculous. The fabliaux about Reynard the Fox are best known today.—Ed.

[7] The Goliards, or wandering scholars, wrote lighthearted Latin verse glorifying pleasure and proclaiming an irreverent attitude toward "the establishment" in twelfth century society.—Ed.

the great center for the study of classical literature, the course of study had been enriched by several new works on geometry, which then embraced so many sciences. . . .

And this brings us to a third characteristic, the practicality of the age. They wanted to apply everything as soon as they learned it. The Cornificians[8] had urged a shorter and more practical course of study. Doubters in religious matters passed into heresy. Reformers were determined to make over Church and civil government. John of Salisbury, the humanist, argued for tyrannicide. The problems involved in building cathedrals were studied and mastered; a new type of architecture, the Gothic, was evolved. This, with its daring conceptions and carefully balanced thrusts, marks two phases of the bourgeois spirit to which it owed its development.

Nowhere was this practical spirit shown more clearly than in the new type of monasticism represented by the Templars, Hospitalers, Bridge-Builders, Premonstratensians, and still more forcibly in the following century by the Franciscans and Dominicans. A new ideal, service to others, had become the dominant feature in the later monasticism.

All of these factors were the product of the restlessness of the age. Men were constantly in motion. Crusades took tens of thousands away from their homes and brought the peoples of Europe into contact with one another. Those who did not go on the crusades or other great expeditions were extremely mobile. The population was not at all stationary, chained to the soil. This was the era of villeneuves,[9] of the growth of older cities, of the great fairs, of the migration of masons from one city to another, of the wandering jongleur and student. "Mixture, or at least contact, of races is essential to progress," and the countries of western Europe, after several centuries of comparative isolation, now experienced the advantages of this mixture or contact. Wealth increased, new tastes were formed and gratified, learning advanced, life became fuller, the spirit of nationality was awakened.

[8] John of Salisbury's term for his opponents who urged a utilitarian approach to education. —Ed.

[9] The new towns being founded as part of "the rise of towns".—Ed.

The publication in 1927 of *The Renaissance of the Twelfth Century* by CHARLES HOMER HASKINS (1870–1937) spread the idea of this renaissance outside a small group of specialists in medieval studies. His brilliant synthesis continues to be widely read and to exert influence by its persuasive argument as well as by its style and captivating title. Haskins spent much of his professional life at Harvard as teacher and Dean of the Graduate School of Arts and Sciences from 1908 to 1924. He played a leading role in the Mediaeval Academy of America, the American Historical Association, and the American Council of Learned Societies. His book on *Norman Institutions* published in 1918 remains a basic work. *Studies in the History of Mediaeval Science* (1924) and *Studies in Mediaeval Culture* (1929) are collections of his specialized articles that underlie his more popular books, such as *The Rise of the Universities* (1923). By confining his investigation of the twelfth-century renaissance to the history of culture, Haskins presented a more precise treatment than Munro and set a pattern that has been followed by most scholars who deal with the subject.*

The Renaissance
of the Twelfth Century

The title of this book will appear to many to contain a flagrant contradiction. A renaissance in the twelfth century! Do not the Middle Ages, that epoch of ignorance, stagnation, and gloom, stand in the sharpest contrast to the light and progress and freedom of the Italian Renaissance which followed? How could there be a renaissance in the Middle Ages, when men had no eye for the joy and beauty and knowledge of this passing world, their gaze ever fixed on the terrors of the world to come? Is not this whole period summed up in Symonds'[1] picture of St. Bernard, blind to the beauties of Lake Leman as he bends "a thought-burdened forehead over the neck of his mule," typical of an age when "humanity had passed, a careful pilgrim, intent on the terrors of sin, death, and

[1] For English readers, John Addington Symonds, *Renaissance in Italy*, appearing in seven volumes from 1875 to 1886, was the most important book in forming their ideas of the Italian Renaissance.—Ed.

judgment, along the highways of the world, and had scarcely known that they were sightworthy, or that life is a blessing"?

The answer is that the continuity of history rejects such sharp and violent contrasts between successive periods, and that modern research shows us the Middle Ages less dark and less static, the Renaissance less bright and less sudden, than was once supposed. The Middle Ages exhibit life and color and change, much eager search after knowledge and beauty, much creative accomplishment in art, in literature, in institutions. The Italian Renaissance was preceded by similar, if less wide-reaching movements; indeed it came out of the Middle Ages so gradually that historians are not agreed when it began, and some would go so far as to abolish the name, and perhaps even the fact, of a renaissance in the Quattrocento [fifteenth century].

To the most important of these earlier revivals the present volume is devoted, the Renaissance of the Twelfth Century which is often called the Mediaeval Renaissance. This century, the very century of St. Bernard and his mule, was in many respects an age of fresh and vigorous life. The epoch of the Crusades, of the rise of towns, and of the earliest bureaucratic states of the West, it saw the culmination of Romanesque art and the beginnings of Gothic; the emergence of the vernacular literatures; the revival of the Latin classics and of Latin poetry and Roman law; the recovery of Greek science, with its Arabic additions, and of much of Greek philosophy; and the origin of the first European universities. The twelfth century left its signature on higher education, on the scholastic philosophy, on European systems of law, on architecture and sculpture, on the liturgical drama, on Latin and vernacular poetry. . . .

The European Middle Ages form a complex and varied as well as a very considerable period of human history. Within their thousand years of time they include a large variety of peoples, institutions, and types of culture, illustrating many processes of historical development and containing the origins of many phases of modern civilization. Contrasts of East and West, of the North and the Mediterranean, of old and new, sacred and profane, ideal and actual, give life and color and movement to this period, while its close relations alike to antiquity and to the modern world assure it a place in the continuous history of human development. Both continuity and change are characteristic of the Middle Ages, as indeed of all great epochs of history.

This conception runs counter to ideas widely prevalent not only among the unlearned but among many who ought to know better. To these the Middle Ages are synonymous with all that is uniform, static, and unprogressive; "mediaeval" is applied to anything outgrown, until, as Bernard Shaw reminds us, even the fashion plates of the preceding generation are pronounced "mediaeval." The barbarism of Goths and Vandals is thus spread out over the following centuries, even to that "Gothic" architecture which is one of the crowning achievements of the constructive genius of the race; the ignorance and superstition of this age are contrasted with the enlightenment of the Renaissance, in strange disregard of the alchemy and demonology which flourished throughout this succeeding period; and the phrase "Dark Ages" is extended to cover all that came between, let us say, 476 and 1453. Even those who realize that the Middle Ages are not "dark" often think of them as uniform, at least during the central period from *ca.* 800 to *ca.* 1300, distinguished by the great mediaeval institutions of feudalism, ecclesiasticism, and scholasticism, and preceded and followed by epochs of more rapid transformation. Such a view ignores the unequal development of different parts of Europe, the great economic changes within this epoch, the influx of the new learning of the East, the shifting currents in the stream of mediaeval life and thought. On the intellectual side, in particular, it neglects the mediaeval revival of the Latin classics and of jurisprudence, the extension of knowledge by the absorption of ancient learning and by observation, and the creative work of these centuries in poetry and in art. In many ways the differences between the Europe of 800 and that of 1300 are greater than the resemblances. Similar contrasts, though on a smaller scale, can be made between the culture of the eighth and the ninth centuries, between conditions *ca.* 1100 and those *ca.* 1200, between the preceding age and the new intellectual currents of the thirteenth and fourteenth centuries.

For convenience' sake it has become common to designate certain of these movements as the Carolingian Renaissance, the Ottonian Renaissance, the Renaissance of the Twelfth Century, after the fashion of the phrase once reserved exclusively for the Italian Renaissance of the fifteenth century. Some, it is true, would give up the word renaissance altogether, as conveying false impressions of a sudden change and an original and distinct culture in the fifteenth century, and, in general, as implying that there ever can be a real revival of something past; Mr. Henry Osborn Taylor prides himself on writing two volumes on *Thought and Expression in the Sixteenth Century* without once using this forbidden term. Nevertheless, it may be doubted whether such a term is more open to misinterpretation than others, like the Quattrocento or the sixteenth century, and it is so convenient and so well established that, like Austria, if it had not existed we should have to invent it. There was an Italian Renaissance, whatever we choose to call it, and nothing is gained by the process which ascribes the Homeric poems to another poet of the same name. But—thus much we must grant— the great Renaissance was not so unique or so decisive as has been supposed. The contrast of culture was not nearly so sharp as it seemed to the humanists and their modern followers, while within the Middle Ages there were intellectual revivals whose influence was not lost to succeeding times, and which partook of the same character as the better known movement of the fifteenth century. To one of these this volume is devoted, the Renaissance of the Twelfth Century, which is also known as the Mediaeval Renaissance.

The renaissance of the twelfth century might conceivably be taken so broadly as to cover all the changes through which Europe passed in the hundred years or more from the late eleventh century to the taking of Constantinople by the Latins in 1204 and the contemporary events which usher in the thirteenth century, just as we speak of the Age of the Renaissance in later Italy; but such a view becomes too wide and vague for any purpose save the general history of the period. More profitably we may limit the phrase to the history of culture in this age—the complete development of Romanesque art and the rise of Gothic; the full bloom of vernacular poetry, both lyric and epic; and the new learning and new literature in Latin. The century begins with the flourishing age of the cathedral schools and closes with the earliest universities already well established at Salerno, Bologna, Paris, Montpellier, and Oxford. It starts with only the bare outlines of the seven liberal arts and ends in possession of the Roman and canon law, the new Aristotle, the new Euclid and Ptolemy, and the Greek and Arabic physicians, thus making possible a new philosophy and a new science. It sees a revival of the Latin classics, of Latin prose, and of Latin verse, both in the ancient style of Hildebert[2] and the new rhymes of the Goliardi, and the formation of the liturgical drama. New activity in historical writing reflects the variety and amplitude of a richer age—biography, memoir, court annals, the vernacular history, and the city chronicle. A library of *ca.* 1100 would have little beyond the Bible and the Latin Fathers, with their Carolingian commentators, the service books of the church and various lives of saints, the textbooks of Boethius [*ca.* 470–*ca.* 525] and some others, bits of local history, and perhaps certain of the Latin classics, too often covered with dust. About 1200, or a few years later, we should expect to find, not only more and better copies of these older works, but also the *Corpus Juris Civilis*[3] and the classics partially rescued from neglect; the canonical collections of Gratian[4] and the recent Popes; the theology of Anselm and Peter Lombard and the other early scholastics; the writings of St. Bernard and other monastic leaders (a good quarter of the two hundred and seventeen volumes of the Latin *Patrologia*[5] belong to this period); a mass of new history, poetry, and correspondence; the philosophy, mathematics, and astronomy unknown to the earlier mediaeval tradition and recovered from the Greeks and Arabs in the course of the twelfth century. We should now have the great feudal epics of France and the best of the Provençal lyrics, as well as the earliest works in Middle High German. Romanesque art would have reached and passed its prime, and the new Gothic style would be firmly established at Paris, Chartres, and lesser centres in the Île de France.

A survey of the whole Western culture of the twelfth century would take us far afield, and in many directions the preliminary studies are still lacking. The limits of the present volume, and of its author's knowledge, compel us to leave aside the architecture and sculpture of the age, as well as its vernacular literature, and concentrate our attention upon the Latin writings of the period and what of its life and thought they reveal. Art and literature are never wholly distinct, and Latin and vernacular cannot, of course, be sharply separated, for they run on lines which are often parallel and often cross or converge, and we are learning that it is quite impossible to maintain the watertight compartments which were once thought to separate the writings of the learned and the unlearned. The interpenetration of these

---

2 Hildebert of Lavardin (*ca.* 1056–1133), sometimes also identified as "of Tours," was a poet whose Latin style was so classical that his works were mistakenly attributed by scholars to the classical period.—Ed.

3 The *Corpus* was the emperor Justinian's great collection of Roman law made in the early sixth century. The part most important for the revived study of Roman civil law that began in the West in the eleventh century was the *Digest*, which contained the opinions of great Roman jurists who developed the principles of Roman law. —Ed.

4 Gratian's *Decretum* (*ca.* 1140), a collection of canon law, became the basis for the study of canon law.—Ed.

5 The standard collection by Joseph Migne of writings of the Church Fathers.—Ed.

two literatures must constantly be kept in mind. Nevertheless, the two are capable of separate discussion, and, since far more attention has been given to the vernacular, justification is not hard to find for a treatment of the more specifically Latin Renaissance.

Chronological limits are not easy to set. Centuries are at best but arbitrary conveniences which must not be permitted to clog or distort our historical thinking: history cannot remain history if sawed off into even lengths of hundreds of years. The most that can be said is that the later eleventh century shows many signs of new life, political, economic, religious, intellectual, for which, like the revival of Roman law and the new interest in the classics, specific dates can rarely be assigned, and that, if we were to choose the First Crusade in 1096 as a convenient turning-point, it must be with a full realization that this particular event has in itself no decisive importance in intellectual history, and that the real change began some fifty years earlier. At the latter end the period is even less sharply defined. Once requickened, intellectual life did not slacken or abruptly change its character. The fourteenth century grows out of the thirteenth as the thirteenth grows out of the twelfth, so that there is no real break between the mediaeval renaissance and the Quattrocento. Dante, an undergraduate once declared, "stands with one foot in the Middle Ages while with the other he salutes the rising star of the Renaissance"! If the signature of the thirteenth century is easy to recognize in the literature, art, and thought of *ca.* 1250, as contrasted with the more fluid and formative epoch which precedes, no sharp line of demarcation separates the two. We can only say that, about the turn of the century, the fall of

the Greek empire, the reception of the new Aristotle, the triumph of logic over letters, and the decline of the creative period in Latin and French poetry, mark a transition which we cannot overlook, while two generations later the new science and philosophy have been reduced to order by Albertus Magnus and Thomas Aquinas. By 1200 the mediaeval renaissance is well advanced, by 1250 its work is largely done. In a phrase like "the renaissance of the twelfth century," the word "century" must be used very loosely so as to cover not only the twelfth century proper but the years which immediately precede and follow, yet with sufficient emphasis on the central period to indicate the outstanding characteristics of its civilization. For the movement as a whole we must really go back fifty years or more and forward almost as far.

Furthermore, the various phases of the movement do not exactly synchronize, just as in the later Renaissance there is not complete parallelism between the revival of classical learning, the outburst of Italian art, and the discoveries of Columbus and Copernicus. Certainly the revival of the Latin classics begins in the eleventh century, if indeed it may not be regarded as a continuous advance since Carolingian times, while the force of the new humanism is largely spent before the twelfth century is over. The new science, on the other hand, does not start before the second quarter of the twelfth century, and once begun it goes on into the thirteenth century in unbroken continuity, at least until the absorption of Greek and Arabic learning is completed. The philosophical revival which starts in the twelfth century has its culmination in the thirteenth. Here, as throughout all history, no single date possesses equal importance in all lines of development.

Unlike the Carolingian Renaissance, the revival of the twelfth century was not the product of a court or a dynasty; and, unlike the Italian Renaissance, it owed its beginning to no single country. If Italy had its part, as regards Roman and canon law and the translations from the Greek, it was not the decisive part, save in the field of law. France, on the whole, was more important, with its monks and philosophers, its cathedral schools culminating in the new University of Paris, its Goliardi and vernacular poets, its central place in the new Gothic art. England and Germany are noteworthy, though in the spread of culture from France and Italy rather than in its origination; indeed, the period in Germany is in some respects one of decline as we approach the thirteenth century, while England moves forward in the closest relation with France, as regards both Latin and vernacular culture. Spain's part was to serve as the chief link with the learning of the Mohammedan world; the very names of the translators who worked there illustrate the European character of the new search for learning: John of Seville, Hugh of Santalla, Plato of Tivoli, Gerard of Cremona, Hermann of Carinthia, Rudolf of Bruges, Robert of Chester, and the rest. Christian Spain was merely a transmitter to the North.

No scholar has given greater emphasis to the twelfth century as a period of change than FRIEDRICH HEER (b. 1916). He draws a sharp contrast between the "open society" of the twelfth and the "closed" Europe of the thirteenth and fourteenth centuries. Although his interpretation may be considered extreme by some scholars, his views, expressed more boldly than is common in scholarly writing, have proved stimulating to scholars and students alike. His method of analysis provides one way of viewing the culture of the twelfth century without isolating it from other developments in the period, as Haskins and those who followed him were in danger of doing. Heer is professor of history at the University of Vienna and specializes in the intellectual history of Europe. His ideas about the twelfth century were first published in his *Aufgang Europas* in 1949; the book from which these selections were taken was originally published in German in 1961.*

▶ *An Open Society*

Our contemporary European societies, both Western and Eastern, in many ways continue to live on their medieval inheritance. History is the present, and the present is history. When we look more closely into the crises and catastrophes, the hopes and fears of our own day, whether we know it or not we are concerned with developments whose origins can be traced back directly or indirectly to their source in the high Middle Ages.

During this period Europe underwent some far-reaching transformations. The continent which in the twelfth century was open and expanding by the mid-fourteenth century had become closed, a Europe of internal and external frontiers, where nations, states, churches (i.e. the various regional "Gallicanized" churches) and intellectual systems already confronted one another—often in uncompromising and hostile attitudes—in the forms they were to retain at least until the mid-nineteenth century or even into the twentieth.

In the twelfth, and to a large extent still in the early thirteenth century, Europe had the characteristics of an open

* Reprinted by permission of The World Publishing Company and Weidenfeld & Nicholson, Ltd. from *The Medieval World* by Friedrich Heer. Copyright 1961 by George Weidenfeld and Nicholson, Ltd. Eng. Transl. Copyright © 1962 by George Weidenfeld and Nicholson. Translated by Janet Sondheimer. Pp. 17–21, 101–104, 116–119.

society. The frontiers, later to become barriers, "iron curtains" delimiting separate worlds, were still open, even fluid. There were open frontiers on Europe's eastern borders. Until the time of the Mongol onslaught and the Fourth Crusade (1204) Russia was still accessible to the West, linked to Western Europe and Germany by commercial and economic ties and by aristocratic intermarriage. In the eleventh and twelfth centuries an international trade route running from Scandinavia to Byzantium passed through the centre of Russia, by way of Novgorod. The magnificent twelfth-century doors of Novgorod cathedral of German workmanship, still stand as witness to this link.

Whilst it was still open, Russia was a bridge across another of Europe's frontiers, that between Byzantium and Rome, between the churches of the East and West. The antithesis between medieval Rome and Byzantium was as ancient as that between Latin and Greek; the two confronted one another as opposites, like the Old Testament prophets and apostles face to face on the façades of medieval cathedrals. Since the eighth century there had been a steady increase in ecclesiastical rivalry between Rome, the city of the Popes, and Constantinople, the city of the Emperor Constantine, "equal of the Apostles." Byzantium, that is to say the Eastern Roman Emperor and the Eastern Church, was highly suspicious of the new Frankish Empire and the support it received from the Papacy. What lay in the balance was the conversion to Christianity of the newly emerging nations of Eastern Europe: whoever achieved it would become the decisive influence in the formation of their political, social and intellectual traditions.

Although in the eleventh century a serious breach occurred in the relations of the Latin and Greek churches, nevertheless the open Europe of the twelfth century still gave scope for friendly intercourse, as the art of Western Europe impressively bears witness. The real break came with the Fourth Crusade and its aftermath. It was this final rupture between the Greek and Latin churches that set Eastern and Western Europe at odds with each other for the next seven centuries. The sight of swarms of Franks ("barbarians," "brigands," "warmongers" are among the terms used to describe them) marching into the Holy Land led by their princes and bishops aroused the cultivated Greek intelligentsia, clerical and lay, to loathing and despair. To the Byzantines it seemed the Franks could have only one objective: the destruction of the world's greatest political and cultural masterpiece, the great Empire of the Rhomaioi, that marvellous and multi-national empire which had so long defended itself against so many enemies.

The third frontier of this open Europe of the twelfth and early thirteenth centuries, that with Islam, was also fluid. True, there was fighting in Spain, which meant that here the aristocracies of the two cultures were constantly in combat. But even so, old friendships prospered and new ones were formed, Islamic and Hispano-Christian families intermarried, and even the Cid Campeador, the greatest Spanish hero in the war with Islam, whose exploits are celebrated in the national epic, spent most of his life in the service of Islamic rulers.

In this expanding Europe of the twelfth century there was such curiosity and so great a thirst for knowledge that the intellectual and cultural treasure Islam had to offer exerted an immense attraction. This treasure was nothing less than the intellectual wealth of Greek antiquity, augmented by the glosses and commentaries of Islamic scholars from the Near East and the Mediterranean, masters in a vast and flourishing "empire of learning" which stretched from Persia and Samarkand by way of Baghdad and Salerno to Toledo. Arab (and Jewish) translators and commentators helped to make the heritage of philosophical and scientific writings left by Plato and Aristotle and their disciples and successors available to the West. Not only in Spain, but also in southern France, Sicily and southern Italy, there were men who welcomed these contacts and kept the lines of communication with Islam open.

If there was room for manoeuvre on these three "external" frontiers of Europe in the twelfth century, there was a corresponding internal flexibility: learning was liberal, popular piety took many forms, the Church itself stood open. Learning was becoming more broadly based. The young clerks who in growing numbers frequented the cathedral schools of France and Germany and the municipal schools of Italy brought with them curiosity, freshness and open minds. The culture they acquired there had many elements derived from pagan antiquity and the non-Christian world of the Orient, strands which threaded themselves into a brightly-coloured tissue to adorn not only the humanism of Chartres but also the courtly culture of the Angevin Empire. This was no mere flash in the pan. The poets and natural philosophers of the Italian Renaissance of the fifteenth and sixteenth centuries had their predecessors in the humanists, Platonists, natural philosophers, poets and theoretical exponents of the *ars amandi* (the art of loving in the courtly, civilized fashion, governed by strict rules) of the twelfth century, who had shown themselves so readily receptive of such alien material. Similarly, in the sixteenth and seventeenth centuries, when the foundations of modern scientific thought were being laid, philosophers and natural scientists (Nicholas of Cues, Leibnitz, Galileo, Isaac Newton, Boyle and Locke) constantly looked back to what had been learned in the open Europe of the twelfth and early thirteenth centuries.

This widely-ranging eclecticism was only possible because of the open-mindedness prevailing in the Church and in religious life as a whole. It is sheer prejudice which condemns the entire Middle Ages as a Dark Age, based on the hackneyed assumption that the medieval mind was narrow, dominated by a fanatical clergy, strait-jacketed by a rigid set of dogmas. Reality presents quite a contrary picture. True, no medieval century (any more than any modern century) was entirely free from intolerance; there were always people full of hatred and mistrust of their neighbours and of anyone who did not conform, there were always people whose hearts and minds were narrow and fearful. But what is important for a proper appreciation of the twelfth and early thirteenth centuries, and of the perspectives then opened up, is to realize that both the pious common folk and the spiritual élite accepted with great readiness, in all the robust and wholesome simplicity of young peoples and young minds, a truly "catholic" religion, compounded of a great variety of elements. It was only when the world turned puritanical that this synthesis was broken, subjected to analysis by purists who sorted out its various components and dug deep chasms to keep them apart. This open religion of the earlier Middle Ages was a satisfying blend of ingredients taken from pre-Christian "pagan" folk religions with others that were certainly Christian but which had acquired an exotic flavouring from their intimate association with contrasting and non-Christian material. This religion, which was the religion of the people and also in some cases that of the ruling classes and of eminent personalities, will be more fully discussed later. All that needs to be stressed here is that it could be accommodated, together with an open culture, within the broad bosom of an equally open Church, in a way which later filled the men of the Reformation and Counter-Reformation with fear and disgust.

The open Church of the open twelfth century permitted liberties that were inconceivable to later generations. This was a living Church, alive in body and members, buoyant, pliable and colourful. The number of the sacraments had not yet been fixed at seven, nor had the Mass reached its final form. Many articles of faith were still without definition as dogmas; they were to be debated by the Schoolmen in the thirteenth century and ultimately defined by the Council of Trent. It was not until the middle of the twelfth century that the Church as an entity was even mentioned. Up to that time people thought rather in terms of Christendom; no-one wrote theological or religio-political treatises on "the Church" ("church" meant the building, the House of God), nor was there much talk of theology. It was the audacious Abelard who introduced theology in its modern sense, both as a word and as a concept, into Europe. As a word it had been avoided for its associations with pagan antiquity; and men were fully conscious of its dangers as a concept, feeling that attempts to "understand" God, to imprison Him within the rigid vice of theology, was a form of temptation. The

theological speculations of this older, more open Europe moved instead about the great mysteries of faith, in an attitude of reticence, reverence and love. This faith, like all ultimate realities, could ultimately only be experienced, never comprehended.

The open Church of the older Europe was a living union of mighty opposites: Heaven and Earth, matter and spirit, living and dead, body and soul, past, present and future. Reality was seamless, there was no chasm separating created from redeemed mankind; all men were of one blood, from the first man to the last, and inhabited a single hemisphere, at once natural and "supernatural." It was not until the thirteenth century that theology was invaded by the concept of the "supernatural." This open Church was served by bishops and lower clergy who led boisterous, cheerful lives, accepting tears and laughter as they came; they were full of *savoir vivre* and very independent in their relations with each other, which were sometimes amicable, sometimes acrimonious. Rome was very remote; so, often, was a man's immediate superior, his bishop or abbot. . . .

Several political and social frontiers which would later be closed still stood open. The long boundary between France and Germany, for centuries one of Europe's worst danger-spots, was in many places nebulous; lordships intermingled there, since many magnates held fiefs and estates both from the French monarchy and the Empire. Within the Empire, Italy only started to pursue its separate interests after its ecclesiastical organization had been disentangled from that of the Empire by the Concordat of Worms in 1122. Europe's eastern frontiers were still quite fluid. The German colonizers and the native

East European nobility (Slavs, Poles, Prussians, Lithuanians and Magyars) were between them bringing Eastern Europe increasingly closer to Central and Western Europe, until together they became a unit, though expansion still continued eastwards into the Baltic. . . .

Everywhere in Western Europe during the twelfth century, in France, Germany, England, Italy and Spain, men's hearts and minds were waking to a new appreciation of the world, its colour, its vastness, its perils and its beauty. There was curiosity about the world in all its aspects, the world of men, the world of the spirit, the world of the cosmos and the world of nature. This was a germinal time, pregnant with a thousand possibilities, and the material and themes treated by the men and women of this age retained a compelling attraction for poets and speculative thinkers right through the Renaissance and Baroque periods and down into the eighteenth century. The twelfth century broke the ground, but the harvest would be reaped by posterity and by men of quite a different temper. There were immeasurable potentialities in the permeation of philosophical, scientific and mystical thought by ideas of alien origin, classical, Arab, Jewish and Oriental (some chronicles actually describe twelfth century Pisa as an "Oriental" city). The first task, and it was undertaken with feverish intensity, was one of translation. The chief centres of this activity were Toledo, Montpellier and a number of Italian towns, from Cremona in the north to Naples and Sicily. Although the bulk of the new material was alien, some of it was in fact long familiar from excerpts in the writings of the Fathers. But this was merely the first breath of fresh air, a pleasurable titillation, some might say

a temptation. Only the high scholasticism of the thirteenth century could make a system out of this alien material.

This readiness to welcome new material was matched by a liberal atmosphere in the schools, where a youthful and enquiring intelligentsia was arming itself mentally and emotionally for the encounter with the hallowed philosophical and poetic giants of the past. Young men of this calibre were to be found in the cathedral schools, particularly those of France (Chartres, Rheims, Laon, Orleans and Paris), and in the earliest universities, at that time still very open and flexible, not to be compared with the rigid, exclusive schools of the later Middle Ages. There were also the "wandering scholars," who were a typical phenomenon of the twelfth century, in which there was so much literary and intellectual movement. These *vagantes*, who were unbeneficed clerks, were acute observers of their times, specialists in satire and irony, and, a few of them, highly gifted poets. Simultaneously, at the first really "courtly" courts known in Europe, great poets were spinning that golden yarn which, although made thin and colourless by incessant handling, has provided material for the novel up to and including our own time.

The twelfth century used Latin both as the instrument of thought and speculation and as the medium of creative imagination. Latin was the speech of the intellectual world throughout Europe, a world at first inhabited exclusively by clerks; and when laymen came to join them they went through the same preliminary education. The Latin of the uncommitted twelfth century was far from being the precise scholars' tongue it was to become when Thomas Aquinas and the thirteenth century schoolmen were wielding it as the chosen instrument of logical, "purely scientific" and juridical thought, when each word was restricted to a single meaning and ever more rigorously and narrowly defined, until it was reduced to a single dimension. The Latin of the twelfth century, and especially the Latin of theologians and philosophers, was a living, flexible language. Each word easily accommodated several layers of meaning, often of great ambivalence. An individual found in this "open" language room to express the religious experience of his childhood, of his people, and of a thousand years of history. Words were still ciphers, symbols, sacraments, a bundling together of different meanings, signposts directing attention to something beyond. The schoolmen of the thirteenth century (and to some extent also of the later twelfth century) had no use for this sort of language: they tore it to pieces and condemned it as "imprecise," "illogical," "unscientific." Yet it was just this kind of language that was eminently suitable for speculative writing and for expressing in all its nuances that spirituality, so instinct with intimations of God and the natural world, which distinguishes some of the most interesting thinkers of the twelfth century.

A preliminary word may be said here about the vernacular literature which was growing up side by side with this "open" Latin. There is magic, in every sense, in the folk poetry of the twelfth century. But the charm of the early vernacular poetry of Spain, Provence, northern France, Germany and the Netherlands soon started to freeze into a polite upper-class diction, strictly limited to a fashionable repertoire in which the language was purged of its "provincial" elements. The vernacular was transformed into the metallic, lucid, somewhat precious language of a social élite of culti-vated people, and this was to set the stage for five centuries of courtly versifying, which all too easily became mannered and pedantic. By the thirteenth century the victory of this self-imprisoned poetic style and of the theological, philosophical and poetic systems which went with it was already assured.

The twelfth century was an open age. In intellectual matters this meant that its touch was sometimes fumbling and uncertain, that problems were attacked hastily before the necessary preliminary work had been done, and that men had an unwarranted confidence in the power of reason, and of numbers, mathematics and geometry, to give decisive answers to the puzzles of the universe. In men of another temperament there was excessive reliance on eloquence, on the virtues of long words and beautifully-turned sentences.

Intellectuals of conservative cast, and they were in the majority, resisted such impetuosity. They included masters of cathedral schools, members of secular orders who were teachers in the new universities, episcopally appointed university chancellors, bishops, and leading theologians and spokesmen of the religious orders. As each new twelfth century thinker appeared, it was very likely that he would soon be surrounded by a crowd of hangers-on, rivals or overt enemies, all concerned, from a variety of motives, to expose him as an "innovator." In narrowly orthodox circles, the main accusation levelled against heretics was that they were innovators, men of the "new truth"; the same charge was to be made five centuries later, at the time of the Counter-Reformation. The German word for heretic, *Ketzer*, is derived from Cathari, meaning "the pure"; and in the twelfth century the whole of south-western Europe had already been penetrated by the teachings of the Cathars, the Waldensians, and a dozen smaller heresies. Thus any twelfth century intellectual, theologian, philosopher or natural philosopher with a taste for speculation found himself engaged simultaneously on three fronts. He had to defend himself from the attacks of his more conservative colleagues, he was expected to resist "heretical" innovators with whom he may well have found himself in some sympathy, and he was likely to be in conflict with colleagues who were "progressives" like himself, but belonged to a different school of thought. Such a situation produced some very complicated relationships and highly dramatic, even tragic, controversies. The lines of the three battlefronts not infrequently became hopelessly entangled: "conservatives" and "innovators" found themselves now allies, now adversaries, without understanding each other's positions. Two characteristics of intellectual controversy now reappeared for the first time since the great Christological debates of the second to fifth centuries: first, the atmosphere of heightened temper and sensibility in which such disputes were conducted, and second, the suspicion and jealousy felt by the participants for each other. This spirit of contention was to stay. The jealousy was all the more bitter in its effects when it was suppressed at the austere dictates of a rigidly disciplined conscience, the natural result of an incomplete awareness of the depths of personality. The twelfth century has its conspicuous examples of *rabies theologica* [theological madness], of the rancour which so often accompanies theological debate, and of the group egoism and vanity found sometimes in religious orders and universities.

The intellectual world of the twelfth century looked both to the past and the future. Looking to the past meant allegiance to the thousand-years-long tradition of a circuitous approach to the mysteries of the triune God, in a spirit of awe and love. Such divine mysteries were "comprehensible" only through symbolism and the reverent interpretation of symbols; they could be revealed to human experience in images and allegory, but might never be completely exposed to view. Looking to the future meant embracing boldly and without prejudice a philosophy which included in one system God, nature, the world and man. . . .

Chartres, and the intellectual activity of the great teachers, friends and scholars associated with its cathedral school, is perhaps the most luminous symbol of the intellectual movement of the twelfth century in all its pristine youthfulness and egregious audacity. Abelard himself may have studied mathematics there under Thierry.

The cathedral school was presided over by two of Abelard's Breton compatriots, the brothers Bernard and Thierry, and by Gilbert de la Porrée. The patron of the school was Godfrey, Bishop of Chartres, an aristocrat from an old Beauce family, a great statesman, a friend of Bernard of Clairvaux, and perhaps a pupil of Abelard. It was he who appointed the three great chancellors of the cathedral school, Bernard, Gilbert and Thierry. The tremendous intellectual influence of the school, which would long outlive the twelfth century, had already spread as far as Sicily and perhaps even into the Islamic world; Chartres itself was very much influenced by Islam. The radiant grandeur of the humanism of the school of Chartres is still there for all to see in the western façade of the cathedral, built during the time of Bishop Godfrey and perhaps the most beautiful of all medieval façades.

In a contemporary letter Thierry of

Chartres is described as "probably the most important philosopher in the whole of Europe." The expression "Europe" is arresting; it is a long time since it was last heard. The concept of Europe as it was understood by the theorists of the Carolingian Empire had died out long before. The Popes started to talk of Europe again in connection with the Crusade. But this quotation introduces us to a new "Europe," the open Europe of the young intelligentsia, eager to take to themselves everything anyone had ever thought at any time concerning God, nature, the cosmos and mankind.

Intellectibilitas, a new word coined at Chartres by Clarenbald,[1] reveals a guiding principle of the school: God, the cosmos, nature and mankind can be examined, reasoned about, comprehended and measured, in their proportions, number, weight and harmony. Clarenbald had another saying: "to theologize is to philosophize." Chartres' essentially Platonic philosophy turned theology into mathematics, geometry. Natural philosophers of the sixteenth to eighteenth centuries, until after the time of Leibnitz, continued to be fascinated by these twelfth century thinkers who found the fundamental principles of reality in the mystery of numbers, the mathematical structure of the cosmos. Thierry explained the Trinity by geometrical symbols, and expounded the nature of God's Son as a rectangle. These preoccupations seem somewhat trivial. They may have stemmed from an atavistic belief in the magical significance of numbers and geometrical figures, or perhaps have been influenced by the Cabala[2] and by Neo-Platonist and Islamic speculation.

[1] Clarenbald of Arras (d. 1170) was a pupil of Thierry of Chartres and Hugh of St. Victor. —Ed.

[2] The Cabala was a cryptic and mystical Jewish work whose first part was given its present form in the ninth century.—Ed.

The element of play cannot be doubted, but with it was combined, and this is more important, a sustained effort at understanding the cosmos in its mathematical structure and at establishing theology as the mother of all the sciences, as something to be established rationally, an art governed by strict logic.

Alain de Lille, a student of Chartres, introduced the logical concept of the axiom into theology, and tried to rethink theology as a logical system. Another student of Chartres, Nicholas of Amiens, dedicated his *Ars Fidei Catholicae* to Pope Clement III; "the catholic faith" (so-called for the first time, since it now had to be distinguished from so many other faiths) was a discipline which could be both taught and learned. Theology was the highest form of arithmetic; in Nicholas' hands it was also fitted into the pattern of Euclidean geometry. The aim was to construct a pellucid, rational theology, light and clear like the Gothic cathedrals, in which the number, light, music and architecture of the cosmos—all based on numerical relationships—showed forth the nature of the Godhead itself. . . .

For the first time in the history of Western European philosophy and poetry we find here the idea of "nature" as cosmic power, the goddess *Natura* (in Goethe's sense), radiant and beguiling, the demonic-divine mother of all things. The small band of scholars of the Chartres school who held this view illustrate the ambivalence of the twelfth century intellectual. Poets, natural philosophers, boldly speculative thinkers, they died as bishops and orthodox churchmen. Their thought, their work, the whole course of their lives would have been impossible even one or two generations later. In Italy and southern France in the sixteenth century men were burned for thinking much less dangerous thoughts than a Bernard Sylvestris or a William of Conches or an Alain de Lille, all members of the twelfth century circle at Chartres. All the same, it should not be forgotten that the members of this small group, as bold as they were learned, were already past masters in the art of Nicodemism: that is to say, dangerous thoughts, dangerous allusions to topical ecclesiastical and political affairs, and above all to ideas hard or impossible to reconcile with the dogma of the Church or the maxims of the prevailing theology, were clothed in symbolical and allegorical forms and put into the mouths of classical poets.

One of the most perceptive books about the Middle Ages, widely accepted as an outstanding synthesis in the field, is *The Making of the Middle Ages* (1953) by RICHARD W. SOUTHERN (b. 1912). His method conveys the spirit of the period by relating typical individuals to the general trends of medieval society, in contrast to the formal categories of analysis used by Heer. By the later twelfth century the work of assimilating ancient culture had been accomplished and a new creative spirit had emerged. Differing from Haskins, who concentrated on writers and thinkers who formed a cultural elite, Southern calls attention to the audience who read their writings Thereby, he gives emphasis to the spread of culture in the twelfth century and shows that culture was no longer confined to a few individuals or to members of an imperial court as in the earlier Middle Ages. Southern is now Chichele Professor of Modern History at Oxford University. His recent writings include *St. Anselm and His Biographer* (1963), an edition of Eadmer's *Vita Anselmi* (1963), and articles on topics of English history in the twelfth century.*

Latin Culture Becomes Widespread

A very different picture [from that of the monastic schools] meets us when we come to consider the communities of secular clergy, and especially the cathedral churches, as centres of learned activity. At first sight, the difference seems to lie chiefly in the deficiencies of the secular bodies. The same impulses are at work, but they work more feebly. In the development of their services, they follow the monasteries, but at a distance. Their libraries were on the whole less exten-sive, the obligation to study less well defined or lacking, the routine of life less regular. The corporate spirit was alive, and it sometimes aroused passionate feelings, but there was less for it to feed on —less to defend in the way of privileges and ancient rights. The individual members of a chapter lived apart, drew their own revenues, farmed their own estates; it was only in moments of crisis that they drew together. In such conditions, the solid achievements of monastic learn-

* From Richard W. Southern, *The Making of the Middle Ages.* (New Haven, Conn.: Yale University Press, 1961), pp. 193–215. Footnotes omitted.

ing are scarcely to be looked for. Even at their best, without the scandals which marked the church at Arezzo, the cathedral bodies were—in the eyes of many reformers of the tenth and eleventh centuries—disorganized and disgraceful bodies. They were strongholds of married clergy; the canons were in the position of monks without monastic discipline; their attendance to their duties in church, for which after all they primarily existed, was difficult or impossible to enforce. There were many attempts to discipline them, as the monasteries were disciplined in the tenth century. Rules were drawn up to give them a common life modelled on the Rule of St. Benedict, and in England, where the alliance between ecclesiastical reformers and secular princes was peculiarly strong and invited strong measures, a considerable proportion of the cathedrals were turned into Benedictine monasteries outright and remained so till the Reformation. But, on the whole, the cathedral chapters proved obdurate. Marriage had to go—the tide against that was too strong. But the other features which made the secular cathedrals hateful to the stern school of reform remained. The great cathedral dignitaries preserved their free, unregulated way of life, mixing their private secular cares—and often high secular office—with their spiritual duties. Throughout the centuries, the cathedrals opposed an obstinate individualism, localism and worldliness to all currents of reform. They were very hard nuts to crack.

What place was there in bodies such as these for the pursuit of learning? It is true that in the ambitious educational projects of the Carolingian age—among which must be reckoned the far-reaching plans for lay education in England attributed to King Alfred—the cathedral

churches were to have had an important part. Numerous councils of the eighth and ninth centuries emphasized the obligation laid on both monasteries and cathedral churches to provide free instruction to all comers. But, so far as the monasteries were concerned, the ideals of later reformers generally discouraged any development of this kind. And, so far as the cathedral churches were concerned, the councils grew weary of reiterating a demand which could not be enforced, and they were silent on this subject for over three centuries. It was not until 1179 that the Third Lateran Council renewed the injunction that all cathedrals should provide a suitable benefice for a master to teach, free of charge, the clerks of the church and other poor scholars. Yet it was during these centuries of legislative silence that the cathedrals made their great contribution to learning. How did this come about?

In the first place, the long silence of legislators could not do away with the need for some form of instruction in the great collegiate churches. The church services had to be maintained and elaborated, following the fashion of the time. Hence there was a need for that same wide range of activities which we have already noticed in connexion with the monastic services. It was not without reason that the precentor, who was responsible for the arrangement and execution of the daily round of services, was in many cathedrals next in importance to the dean. Then there were letters to be written and business to be transacted on behalf of the chapter which required gifts of scholarship and a fine knowledge of law. The dignitary who was responsible for writing the chapter's letters and keeping its correspondence was also, in many cases, responsible for directing the school. We may suspect that this often took second place to his other duties. Organically the school had only a small place in the cathedral organization, but it could scarcely be omitted altogether.

In all this, however, we are still far from anything that could give the cathedral schools a title to fame. The impulse which raised some of them to heights of scholarly repute came from a larger world than that of ecclesiastical routine. It came from the intellectual restlessness, the desire to know more than the needs of daily life required or than local schoolmasters provided, which seems to strike us as a new factor in the general life of Western Europe as we turn from the tenth to the eleventh century. Certainly in the eleventh century there was a more general interest in intellectual questions than there had been previously. No doubt this only means that an easing of the material conditions of life gave more people a chance for satisfying their intellectual curiosity; but the effect of this was to add a new quality of widespread discussion and dispute, which distinguishes the period from the eleventh century onwards sharply from the preceding age. We have only to notice the different atmosphere of the very technical Eucharistic dispute in the mid-eleventh century as compared with the theological disputes of the ninth century to see the different conditions of intellectual controversy. In the earlier century we find scholars disputing among themselves, often with passion and vindictiveness, but still rather remotely, in a court circle, under the eye of an Emperor, with leisured rotundity of phrase, slowly wielding the heavy bludgeon of authority. The eleventh-century disputants, on the other hand, come into the arena like matadors, armed with the sharp sword of logical distinctions—and, what is more, cheered on by a crowd of supporters,

pupils and colleagues. The eleventh-century scholar in controversy felt himself the representative of a school or a party, he appealed to provincial loyalties; he might easily find himself an object of popular hostility if his views were known to be unorthodox. It is in the eleventh century that we have the beginnings of popular heresies, and the beginnings also of popular persecutions. The teaching of the Church was beginning to stir a lively response at all levels of society.

Another aspect of the change was the rapid growth in the floating population of students of all ages and conditions, prepared to go anywhere for the sake of learning. Such men had always existed, but they now became sufficiently numerous to form a class by themselves, to influence the growth of institutions, and to make it possible to see "trends" in their movements. The most significant of these trends is one which is noticeable from the end of the tenth century in the form of a persistent trickle of able men from Italy to Northern France. So far as we can see they were simply responding to an intellectual pull, similar to that which has drawn artists to Paris during the last hundred years. They left a society, on the whole, more comfortable and more literate for one which was cruder and more aggressive, in search of a learning which was not to be found in Italy. It is a surprising spectacle, for Italy had much to give. It was the home of an active legal science which could trace a faint but sure descent from Roman law. It had schools of learned legists, and the art of rhetoric was cultivated to a high degree. It boasted of the literacy of its laity. But there were things to be learnt in Northern France which satisfied intellectual aspirations, far beyond the range of the legal sciences of Italian communal life or the requirements of monastic routine. It was the desire to learn logic which brought Gerbert [946–1003] from Rome to Rheims; it was a desire to turn from law to grammar and logic which later drew Lanfranc [d. 1089] from Pavia to Tours. These were the subjects in which intellectual novelties and excitements were to be found.

The abundance of scholars created a demand for teachers. Teaching—it is hard to believe it, but it seems to be true—became a road to profit as well as fame. It was noted that Lanfranc, when he became a monk of Bec in about 1040, gave up a profitable career as a free-lance teacher to sink himself in an obscure monastic community. Still more, that prince of free-lance teachers, Abelard, could find audiences, and profitable ones, wherever he chose to teach. But the cathedrals provided a natural focus for the activities of such men. The very great might be able to stand alone in the world and draw the world to them; but the not-so-great would prefer the security of an established institution and a ready-made audience. Cathedrals had libraries; they had schools, however dim; they offered the chance of an assured position, and of advancement to positions of high dignity and emolument. They drew to themselves activities which they did not create, and which no amount of legislating could have created within them. By their stability, they could serve a purpose which no other institution of the time was capable of serving—that of organizing and giving continuity to the keen but wayward impulses which were sending men through many countries and many vicissitudes in search of learning. In doing this, the cathedrals were helped by the very circumstance which had appeared to work against them as

serious centres of study—the slenderness of the connexion between the work of the schools and the life of the cathedral body. It was easy for the cathedral schools to start a life of their own which reflected the changing interests, and drew on the energies, of the outside world.

We may here pause to consider a figure who in a remarkable way drew out the resources inherent in the cathedral body as a centre of learning in the eleventh century. Fulbert, Chancellor and later (1006–28) Bishop of Chartres, is the patriarch among the masters of the great cathedral schools. He was the first to form a school with a distinctive tradition which persisted long after his death. Without himself writing anything great, or starting any new line of thought, he was able, by his sensitivity to what was going on round him, by his encouragement, and his genius for drawing men to him, to make the school of Chartres the most vigorous in Europe. In range of interests and in influence his only immediate predecessor was Gerbert. But Gerbert, despite the powerful impetus he gave to learning, founded no school; except for the excellent Richer, men did not boast that they were his pupils. It is in the society which Fulbert gathered round him at Chartres that we catch our first glimpse of those intimate and affectionate relations between master and pupils, and of that bond of common loyalty uniting the pupils of an outstanding master, which were the peculiar strength of the great medieval schools. After Fulbert, many masters— St. Bruno, Anselm of Laon, Abelard, Gilbert de la Porrée, Peter Lombard and others—won this same kind of loyalty, which kept their memories and their doctrines alive; but more than any of them Fulbert lived in his pupils.

There are many testimonies to the fact that Fulbert's memory was kept alive by his pupils almost to the end of the century, but the most touching of them is the earliest. Fulbert had a pupil from Liége called Adelman, who became Bishop of Brescia towards the end of his life and died in 1057. Shortly after Fulbert's death, he wrote a poem to commemorate the master and eleven of his disciples who had all died within a few years. It is an awkward poem because it followed an old fashion of starting each verse with a different letter arranged in alphabetical order, but through all the uneasiness of diction it glows with a warm sincerity and sense of past glories. Of Fulbert himself, it says:

With what dignity of spiritual interpretation, with what weight of literal sense, with what sweetness of speech, did he expound the deep secrets of philosophy. The studies of Gaul flourished while he taught. He cultivated both human and sacred sciences, and never allowed virtue to be oppressed by poverty. Like a spring dividing into many streams, or a fire throwing off many sparks, so he propagated himself through his pupils in many different sciences.

Then the poet described Fulbert's pupils and their attainments: Hildegar, philosopher, physician and mathematician, who copied the master's habits of manner and speech; Ralph, more a friend of letters than a learned man himself, who had risen from obscurity to an eminent position at Orleans; Engelbert and Lambert, who coming from a poor nest taught for money at Paris and Orleans; Reginald of Tours, a distinguished grammarian; Gerard who went to Jerusalem and died at Verdun on his return; Walter, who scoured Europe for learning and died by violence at Besançon; Reginbald of Cologne, a man of powerful mind and wide fame, who taught Latin to the barbarians of the Rhine; Odulf, Alestan and Gerard, all of Liége, who had helped to maintain the scholastic fame of that city and died before their time.

These men, who died young, were not the most distinguished of Fulbert's pupils: that distinction belongs to Berengar of Tours. Like many of Fulbert's pupils he would have called himself a grammarian—that is to say, he was interested in the meanings and derivations of words, in the relation between language and reality, and in the rules of eloquence. Of his eloquence, which is well-attested, we have little evidence; but that he was a fanatical speculative grammarian, anxious to push the conclusions of his subject as far as possible and to apply them to the clarifying of dogma, there can be no doubt. In this, he broke away from the temper of Fulbert's school with its many-sided interests and its reticence on dogmatic questions, and embodied the more combative spirit of a later age. Fulbert had been dead for twenty years before the implications of Berengar's teaching on the doctrine of the Eucharist began to be widely discussed. At this time, the faithful Adelman was teaching at Speyer, and he heard only distant reports of Berengar's controversial statements. It was many years since he had written the poem in honour of Fulbert and his pupils, but he felt he was the guardian of a tradition, and he wrote to Berengar begging him, *per suavissimam memoriam Fulberti* [by the sweetest memory of Fulbert], to preserve the peace of the Christian commonwealth. He recalled "that most sweet fraternity which they enjoyed under the venerable Socrates of the Academy at Chartres" and charged him to remember the intimate evening conversations in the little garden by the city chapel, in which Fulbert had begged them with tears to keep the royal road marked out by the Fathers before them. It was probably to accompany this letter, and to enforce this plea, that he revised the old poem—substituting a distinguished musician, Sigo, for the colourless and doubtless long forgotten Ralph "more a friend of letters than a learned man himself"—and sent it off to Berengar. Berengar was not quite insensible to Fulbert's claims, for he quoted his authority for his views, but he was a better poet than Adelman, a better grammarian than Fulbert, and too sure of himself for reproof. He labelled Adelman's painful effort a *ridiculus mus* [ridiculous mouse], and made some ironical jest on the author's name, of which the sense is now lost.

A proud man would be apt to treat an appeal to the memory of school-days in this way, and Berengar, with all his piety and liberality, was proud. He was more brilliant than Fulbert, and he had the power of setting men by the ears and starting them discussing an old question in a new way: as one contemporary wrote to the Pope, the question he started "so filled the world that not only clerks and monks, whose job it is to watch over such matters, but even the laity talked about it among themselves in the streets." But he lacked the benevolent wisdom of Fulbert, which enabled him to form a school at Chartres faithful to his general temper of mind for over a hundred years. Fulbert had a way of saying things which were remembered. The cathedral chapter testified that he was accustomed to speak to them in their distresses *constanter et comfortatorie*; he gave the impression that everything was under control. In all things, except where justice was concerned, he was on the side of moderation. His advice to his

favourite pupil Hildegar when he became Treasurer at Poitiers is typical of his whole teaching: Hildegar was to divide his time between reading, prayer and teaching, and to look after the health of his pupils as well as their minds; he was to remember to care for the orchards and vineyards; he was to allow the church to retain the additional psalms which (here, as elsewhere) had crept into the service, though in Fulbert's view they were superfluous; and the letter concludes with an exposition of the symbolic meaning of some ecclesiastical ornaments, the solution of a small point of Canon Law, some advice on the teaching of grammar, and some books which had been asked for—Cyprian, Porphyry and the Lives of the Fathers.

Fulbert gave a stronger impetus to the development of a school than anyone before the beginning of the twelfth century. He was only able to do this because he was at ease, not only with his Chapter, his pupils and the ideas of his time, but also with the society around him. One can scarcely help comparing him in this respect with Gerbert, who in all probability had been his master. Gerbert was at home only in the past—a limitation which gave strength to his scholarship. But Fulbert entered into the small world of local affairs and personal relationships with the ease of a man at home in the present. He entered into the spirit, and examined the theory, of feudal relationships with a care which Gerbert reserved for the theory of the Empire. His brief exposition of the duties of a vassal to his lord became a classic and was copied more often than any of his works, except those which found a place in the service books of the Church. The correspondence of both Gerbert and Fulbert has been preserved, and to pass from one to the other is to pass from scenes of high life and somewhat artificial political intrigue to the problems of a society of country gentlemen, rough and violent as they were. Men felt that Fulbert was one of themselves, while Gerbert, for all his influence as a scholar, was an alien. The contrast was seized on with customary violence in popular legend, which portrayed Gerbert as a magician who had sold his soul to the devil and penetrated unlawful secrets, while Fulbert came down in tradition as the man who had been cured in illness by the Virgin's milk.

It is worth insisting on Fulbert's easy familiarity with the world, because this was the quality which the cathedral schools were able to add to learning. They brought learned problems—as distinct from problems of religious observance—home to a wide circle of men living in the world. It is doubtful whether Fulbert added anything to the sum of knowledge, but he touched every side of learning, and everything that he touched he made familiar. The range is important. He was in touch with the latest developments in the sciences of logic, arithmetic and astronomy, which reached Chartres from Rheims in the North-West and from Moslem Spain, and he wrote poems to familiarize his pupils with the processes of calculation and the Arabic names of the stars just coming into fashion. It was a simple form of instruction he practised, suitable to the rudimentary state of the sciences. In early life he was famous as a physician, and it is in keeping with the rest of his work that his fame rested on a large assortment of medicines intelligently applied, rather than on an armoury of difficult words and abstruse theory. There seemed to be no end to his versatility. Like other scholars immersed in the routine of a great church, he composed many pieces for the adornment of the church services—hymns, sequences, and homiles, and (most famous of all) the lessons for the Nativity of the Virgin which were adopted universally throughout the western Church. But if his learning had one foot in the Church, it had the other in a world of new problems. The point may be illustrated by a single incident.

One of the most curious testimonies to the learned interests of the early eleventh century is a small collection of letters which passed between two learned men of the cathedral cities of Liége and Cologne, the former called Ralph, the latter Reginbald. The letters are chiefly concerned with mathematical problems. The writers were not mathematicians in any specialized sense, but like Fulbert and other scholars of the day they took every field of knowledge for their sphere. They had been reading some of the books of logic which were then becoming part of the school curriculum, and here they found remarks which baffled them. Boethius, in one of his Commentaries on Aristotle, had mentioned that the interior angles of a triangle are equal to two right angles. Everyone will recognize the familiar theorem, and it comes as rather a shock—a forcible reminder of the vast scientific ignorance with which the age was faced—that these scholars had no idea what was meant by the interior angles of a triangle. Reginbald had formed the view that they were the angles produced by a line dropped from one of the angles to the opposite side of the triangle, and he recalled that once when he had been passing through Chartres he had taken the problem to Fulbert. He claimed that, after many talks, he had finally convinced Fulbert by his arguments. Whether this was so or not, the story illustrates the scientific gropings of the time, the intercourse between scholars, and the authority of Fulbert in a field where he was as much at sea as his contemporaries. This is only one of the strange misconceptions revealed in these letters, but it is perhaps more important that they also contain the first mention in the West of one of the important scientific novelties of the day, the instrument which had been developed by the Arabs and now (under the name of the astrolabe) was beginning to be known in the Latin world. This also must have been known to Fulbert in his watch-tower at Chartres—it has even been suggested that it was at Chartres that Ralph and Reginbald became acquainted with the astrolabe. Of this we have no evidence, but we may see a distant working of Fulbert's influence in the fact that Chartres remained a centre for the diffusion of Arabic science in the West until well into the twelfth century —and not for diffusion only, but for the most successful absorption of this science into the body of Christian learning which was achieved at any time before the thirteenth century.

A hundred years later a correspondence like that of Ralph and Reginbald would scarcely deserve mention. It is full of crudities, but it shows that problems were being discussed, and lines of enquiry reopened, which had been closed for nearly five hundred years. And though they were being reopened at a level of ignorance which would have confounded Boethius, the letters have the distant promise of an advance beyond the formidable barrier of ancient learning: the astrolabe was an instrument which had not been known in classical times, and its possession made possible a new beginning in the art of astronomical measurement. It is a small sign,

but an important one, opening up a vista of a range of learning not derived from the past.

It was in the school of Chartres that a successor of Fulbert, the great scholar Bernard (Chancellor of Chartres from about 1119 to 1126), coined a phrase which sums up the quality of the cathedral schools in the history of learning, and indeed characterizes the age which opened with Gerbert and Fulbert and closed in the first quarter of the twelfth century with Abelard. He said that the modern scholar, compared with the ancients, was as a dwarf standing on the shoulders of a giant. This is not a great claim; neither, however, is it an example of abasement before the shrine of antiquity. It is a very shrewd and just remark, and the important and original point was that the dwarf *could* see a little farther than the giant. That this was possible was above all due to the cathedral schools, with their lack of a well-rooted tradition and their freedom from a clearly defined routine of study. One must not press the distinction between the learned traditions of cathedrals and monasteries too far—their influence on each other remained strong throughout the eleventh century; but if the image of the bee collecting nectar from many flowers happily expressed the aim of the Benedictine scholar, Bernard's phrase equally happily expressed the aim of a man viewing the world of learning from the greatest of all the cathedral schools.

Fulbert's influence, as a perceptible force in the world of learned men, lasted for just over a century. In the first thirty years of the twelfth century Orderic Vitalis and William of Malmesbury could still write of Bishop Fulbert as a founder of a familiar tradition; somewhat as an Oxford historian might now speak of

Bishop Stubbs. When they were writing, they would have found Fulbert's tolerant and humane spirit still alive at Chartres, and in other cathedrals and monasteries they could have found copies of his literary works. Fulbert, it would seem, had not attached much importance to these—he was a teacher not a writer—and he left his "papers" in confusion when he died. They were collected by two devoted pupils and enjoyed a modest success in the schools of Northern France. But the time came when, except for those compositions which had found a home in the service books of the Church, they ceased to be copied. The learning which they represented, the problems with which they dealt, even the style in which they were written, belonged to a past age. With St. Bernard, Abelard and Hugh of St. Victor, new and commanding figures of more fertile genius than that of Fulbert had appeared; and even masters of smaller stature, like the brothers Anselm and Ralph at Laon, had advanced far beyond the limits of technical achievement which had been possible in the early eleventh century.

It is never possible to say without qualification that the learning of the past—especially of so distant a past as that of Greece and Rome—has been assimilated; that we come to a point where scholars begin to feel comfortable about their command of the achievement of the past. This is the point which we reach in the second generation of the twelfth century. The past still had many shocks in store for Western scholars, and in the last years of our period the intellectual scene was being troubled—more deeply troubled than ever before—by the appearance in Latin versions of the metaphysical and scientific works of Aristotle and his Arabic commentators. These last discoveries open up a new era in western thought and learning, with which we are not here concerned. Throughout the greater part of the twelfth century there was a confident sense that the steady mastery of the works of the past was reaching its natural end.

It became possible at this time to envisage the consolidation of great tracts of knowledge in systematic form. Out of the endless glossing of ancient books there was emerging a view of large subjects, long obscured by a multiplicity of details. The word which came to be used with increasing frequency from the early twelfth century onwards to express this ideal ordering of knowledge was the word *Summa*. The idea of an outline of knowledge is not one which excites many people today: perhaps Mr. H. G. Wells has come nearest to feeling the same sort of excitement about it that twelfth-century scholars felt. To them it was certainly of absorbing interest, and every subject came under the influence of this enthusiasm for system. Indeed the idea sprang naturally from the efforts of eleventh-century scholars, and it expressed the sense which men had of mastering their past. More than that (since from the shoulders of the giants they could see a little farther than their predecessors), the *Summa* was an instrument for the advancement of knowledge: from the beginning it was alive with discussion.

Throughout the century there appeared a succession of works in many fields of study which summed up the learning of the past and, in doing so, became the basis of new enquiries and disputes. In theology there were the *Four Books of Sentences* of Peter Lombard (c. 1150); in canon law the *Decretum* or, more exactly, the *Concordance of Discordant Canons* of Gratian (c. 1140); in

Biblical studies the standard gloss or *Glossa Ordinaria* of the school of Anselm of Laon (c. 1120) and the *Historia Scholastica* of Petrus Comestor (c. 1170); in grammar the *Summa* of Petrus Helias (c. 1140); in rhetoric a number of *Summae* or *Summulae* from the schools of Bologna and the valley of the Loire. These works took their place alongside those of the ancients as the text-books of the medieval universities. They had, for their period, a kind of finality which, without the need for any official recognition, won them a lasting place in the curriculum of European studies. Compared with the school-books produced in the previous century, they had an extraordinarily long life, and the end of their undisputed usefulness in the seventeenth century marks the end of the Middle Ages more decisively than the Renaissance or Reformation.

The central books in this movement towards consolidation of the past were the works of Gratian in Canon Law and Peter Lombard in Theology. Although produced by different authors and in different countries—the one in Bologna and the other in Paris—they must be looked on as the fruits of a single effort. Indeed the effort running through all these works of consolidation is, in a sense, one; but the unity, the similarity of the problems, and the community of thought about the means for solving them, are clearer in these two works than in any of the others. In its graphic way, the legendary tradition of the Middle Ages recognized this unity of effort by picturing Gratian, Peter Lombard and Peter Comestor, the author of the *Historia Scholastica*, as sons of the same mother. The truth is not quite so simple as this, but the legend expresses a truth.

Gratian and Peter Lombard were both teachers, and their great works were the by-products of a long teaching activity. They both ministered to practical needs, for in canon law the need for a general text-book to replace the many incomplete, inadequate or merely local text-books of the previous hundred and fifty years was urgent; and in theology, not only were the needs of students to be considered, but the needs also of Church at large, harried by new opinions and movements of doubtful tendency. The *Sentences* and the *Decretum* were books of the schools, but they looked out on to the world. In every way, their appearance was a work of conciliation: conciliation between the discordant testimonies of the past, conciliation between the accumulated riches of the past and the sharp questionings of the present, conciliation between the dialectical and authoritarian tendencies of their age.

Peter Lombard is the chief representative of this comprehensive and conciliatory spirit. He was the heir of the two chief traditions of scholarship in Europe —the legal learning of Northern Italy, and the dialectical and theological learning of Northern France. He was, as his name suggests, an Italian, and his early and middle years were spent in the schools of Northern Italy. Here he would be familiar with the latest developments in the study of Canon Law, and particularly with the work of Gratian. Perhaps when he left Italy about 1140 he brought with him one of the earliest copies of Gratian's book; and when he died he left a copy to the Cathedral library in Paris. It was St. Bernard who was responsible for introducing him to Paris; and here also it was the Lombard's task to mediate between two worlds. In Bologna he would have felt the influence of Abelard, and he must have been conscious of it even more strongly in Paris. The *Sentences* are a fulfilment of a plan of study which Abelard had adumbrated in his *Sic et Non*; they draw largely on Abelard's work. Yet it was St. Bernard who set Peter Lombard on his way as a theologian: he was St. Bernard's positive contribution to the development of scholastic theology. Amid so much that must be deplored in the controversy between those great men, here at least is the suggestion of a way of peace and ultimate reconciliation.

The Lombard, on his side, entered with grave and sober understanding into the bewildering and often light-headed controversies of the time, and in his *Sentences* we see him steering his way from one question to another as the arguments of the day suggested: "At this point it is customary to enquire. . . . Another point which seems worthy of investigation. . . . Certain men have here been inclined to ask. . . ." With such phrases he makes his way through the maze of contemporary argument. His task was to provide material for discussion, not to stifle it. Under the placid exterior of a text-book, the *Sentences* are alive with the intense and questioning intellectual life of the time. In many ways it was not a very attractive intellectual life: little men with little dialectical gimlets were offering to open all the safes in the theological world. It was this which had alarmed St. Bernard; but Peter Lombard shows no trace of apprehension or indignation at the questions which were asked. "There is," he wrote, "perpetual war between the assertion of the truth and the defence of our own fancies. Therefore with much sweat and labour I have put together this volume of testimonies of eternal truth, to stop the mouths of those who are hateful to God, lest the poison of their wickedness should be poured out on others." This sounds repressive, but in the middle of the twelfth century,

the quoting of authorities was the opening of a debate, not the end of it, and almost every section of the Lombard's book invited debate.

The *Sentences* were a tract for the times; they ministered to the needs of the moment. But they were also a source-book arranged with brilliant clarity and perspicacity. In this respect they had a long descent from the innumerable books of excerpts which had occupied the studious leisure of monastic scholars for centuries. In the meticulous sub-division of the material, they bear the mark of a new age in scholarship, but they present material which for the most part had been chewed over for a very long time. Yet they were not, as the monastic *florilegia* were, a personal record of a life-time's reading: they were a collection made for the purposes of the teacher and the pupil, to fill (as we should say) a gap. The book was made "so that the enquirer in future will not need to turn over an immense quantity of books, since he will find here offered to him without his labour, briefly collected together, what he needs." Here indeed was mastery of the past.

Peter Lombard taught quietly in Paris for nearly twenty years. In 1159, he became Bishop of Paris; he died in 1160. By the time of his death the scholastic map of Europe was beginning to take on the outlines which it retained till the fourteenth century. From the point of view of a young man beginning his career in 1160, the great difference in the situation, as compared with the position at the beginning of our period, was that he knew where to go to get the instruction he required, and he knew that he would be able to make use of it when he had got it. Gerbert's career as a scholar had been one of chance encounters: a chance visit of a pilgrim to his monastery at

Aurillac took him to the Spanish March where it was believed that learned men were to be found; a chance visit of the Count of Barcelona to Rome brought him to the notice of the Pope, who kept him in Italy to teach arithmetic and astronomy; the chance visit of a scholar from Rheims showed him where logic was to be learnt and brought him to Northern Europe; the chance which made him Abbot of Bobbio gave him the run of an ancient library; and he was always dependent on chance correspondents for his knowledge of new books. All this was different for a young man starting his career in the middle of the twelfth century. For those who had not the money to travel far, there were the cathedral schools. He would be an unlucky man who had to travel more than a hundred miles to find one of moderate proficiency, and in many there were teachers of distinction. But above these schools of temporary repute, a few great schools were emerging, whose reputation did not depend on that of a single master, or even on a continued succession of single masters. Among the provincial centres, Chartres, Tours and Orleans still maintained a gallant struggle for pre-eminence in literary studies; but it was not to them that well-to-do or hard-headed students, eager for the advancement which could come from learning, were most likely to turn. They went for preference to places where there was a wider choice of masters and where subjects could be studied which led more directly to places of eminence in royal or episcopal service. Paris and Bologna were the scholastic summits of Europe, and they drew a crowd of students from every nation in Europe. There were of course adventurous spirits, of an importance out of proportion to their numbers, who sought those dangerous founts of new scientific ideas at Toledo or at the medical centres of Salerno and Montpellier. But whether he were timid or bold, a practical man in search of instruction or a scholar in search of inspiration, the mid-twelfth-century student knew his way about.

He not only knew where to study, he also knew that his studies would have a market value. This is the second great contrast with his predecessor of Gerbert's day. Like most modern graduates, the great majority of students in the late twelfth century who made any name for themselves became men of affairs—they did not become country gentlemen or country parsons, and very few spent their lives as teachers; in one form or another they became occupied in administrative work. The importance to government of this marriage with learning has already been mentioned, and a word must now be said about the influence of government on learning. The masters in the schools pursued their task of systematization, elaboration of detail and popularization: on the whole, it was a task in which during the second half of the twelfth century there were few great discoveries or excitements. By the nature of their task, the scholars of the second half of the century seemed to lack the creative power of those in the first half. But on the fringe of the learned world, drawing their power from the learning of the schools and their problems and incidents from the world of affairs, there were some of the most interesting and varied groups of writers which the Middle Ages produced. England, with its rapidly developing government and intense preoccupation with administration from the king's court downwards, was a great place for such men. John of Salisbury, Peter of Blois, Walter Map, Giraldus Cambrensis, and the authors of the first books on the practice of secular government—the *Dialogue of the Exchequer* and the *Treatise on the Laws and Customs of England*—all, in different ways, brought the learning of the schools to bear on the business of the world. As writers, none of them reaches the very first rank; but their appearance marks the full domestication of learning in the West. As we see it now, the intellectual world of Gerbert and Fulbert had been a very small one. Scholars learned with difficulty the elements of sciences to a schoolboy level, and they stretched out painfully beyond the learned needs of small religious communities. Slowly the range of learning transmitted from the ancient world had been mastered. This was the first task, and at the end of the twelfth century only those in touch with the Greek and Moslem world knew how far they were from having completed even this task in the fields of the natural sciences and philosophy. Fortunately perhaps most scholars felt more comfortable about the past than they had any right to feel; and they knew that they lived in a large world of knowledge and achievement.

We may illustrate the new conditions of study and learning, the market for learned men and a scholar's reaction to the world, in the person of one of the writers who found a home in England during the last thirty years of the twelfth century.

Peter of Blois was the son of a minor nobleman of the Loire valley, with the wide family connexions which even minor aristocracy carried with it, but without any prospects in the world except those which he could make for himself. His situation was one which required exertion if it were to be improved, and his quick and lively mind indicated that, for him, the path of promotion lay through the schools rather than along the road of military service. The chronology of his early life is quite uncertain, but at some time about 1160, when he must have been between fifteen and twenty years old, we find him studying at Tours. It was here that he probably first showed his high talent as a poet, and there is no doubt that if he had been content to knock about the world in a more or less disreputable way he would have made his reputation as a poet. He was known to connoisseurs, then as now, as one of the masters of the new poetic idiom, and he handled the complicated forms of the lyric with an easy and subtle grace. But he was too ambitious, and also—to do him justice—too serious, to be content with this success. None of his early poems have come down to us, or if they have they are cloaked in anonymity; he tells us that they were lascivious and it is very probable that they were. But he also tells us that he turned to higher things, and this meant, in the first place, the study of law at Bologna and then theology at Paris. At Bologna, the thing which delighted him most, coming from his literary studies in Tours, was the rhetoric of the law with its amplitude and sonority of words; the technicalities of the law, whether Roman or Canon, seem to have had little attraction for him. Once more, however, he became dissatisfied, and he abandoned law for theology, Bologna for Paris. We do not know who his masters were in Paris, but he must have listened to a good deal of technical discussion, for very late in life—in the early years of the thirteenth century—he turned up his theological notes from Parisian days and thought sufficiently highly of them to reproduce their arguments in his letters.

But he had no intention of becoming a theologian, and by 1167 he was looking round for a job. This was a delicate business. Everything depended on making the right contacts, and he had many disappointments and vexations before he achieved an enviable security as archdeacon of Bath and a man of importance in the household of two successive archbishops of Canterbury. He had hoped for more; but, still, to be an archdeacon and to hold canonries in four or five cathedral churches was comfortable, if not glorious; and he owed the position entirely to his own abilities, in a strange land, with no family influence. Moreover he was among a very interesting set of people. His real work lay not in his archdeaconry, which must for years on end have been left to the care of a deputy, but in the circle of the archbishops of Canterbury, whom he served for twenty years. These were the years after the murder of archbishop Thomas Becket when the relations between the English Church and the Papacy, and between royal and episcopal jurisdiction, were being worked out in detail. There was need of men of talent and education, and they took themselves very seriously. Peter of Blois must have met every man of importance in the kingdom during his twenty years with the archbishops Richard and Baldwin. He wrote many of their letters, and conducted negotiations for them at the royal court or at Rome or with the troublesome monks of Canterbury. Not without reason, he thought himself too great a man to accept the small bishopric of Rochester.

Peter of Blois was one of the most distinguished of the learned men who devoted their learning and talents to the work of administration in the late twelfth century, and he was conscious of the dignity of government. But in moments of repentance he made no secret of the motives which had induced

him to turn his energies in this direction:

I was led by the spirit of ambition and immersed myself entirely in the waves of the world. I put God, the Church and my Order behind me and set myself to gather what riches I could, rather than to take what God sent. Forgetting those things which were behind, I reached forth (but not as the Apostle did) to those things which were before. (Phil. iii, 13) . . . Ambition made me drunk, and the flattering promises of our Prince overthrew me.[1]

When he wrote this, he had just recovered from a dangerous illness and he was full of repentance. He was not always so; but he was never quite at ease in the busy and competitive life of a court. He could not forget that he was a scholar and seriously a Christian, and his illness made him determine to put aside his ambitions and to break off his connexions with the royal court:

In being scourged by the Lord, I received the grace of fatherly correction. I communed with my heart in the night season and searched out my spirit, and I decided to leave this way of life, as Joseph his garment, Matthew his receipt of custom, John his linen cloth, the woman of Samaria her water-pot of avarice. The Lord heard me, and the dew of the divine mercy quenched the flame of ambition, which rivers of silver and gold had formerly been unable to restrain. Stablish the thing, O God, that thou hast wrought in me; permit me not to return to my vomit, nor ever to rebuild the Jericho I have destroyed.

Once recovered, Peter retracted some of the severe things which he had said about the administrative life, and . . . painted the other side of the picture.

[1] For a short time Peter was one of the clerics and men of letters who served at the court of Henry II, king of England (1154–1189), as clerks in his administrative departments. John of Salisbury also was briefly at Henry's court.—Ed.

I do not condemn the life of civil servants, who even if they cannot have leisure for prayer and contemplation, are nevertheless occupied in the public good and often perform works of salvation. All men cannot follow the narrower path—for the way of the Lord is a strait and arduous road, and it is good if those who cannot ascend the mountain can accompany Lot to be saved in the little city of Zoar. . . . I think it is not only laudable but glorious to assist the king, to hold office in the State, not to think of oneself, but to be all for all. But no one shall be involved, and none shall be extricated, from curial chains by me. For Joshua gave the children of Israel a choice, whether to serve the gods of Mesopotamia and the gods of the Amorites, or the Lord God; being willing that none should bear the yoke of service except by his own choice.

He was indeed, as he recognized, not always consistent, and in his different moods he reflected many aspects of his time and the thoughts of many other men. He was sensitive and impulsive, and perhaps after his outburst he would have liked to make his way back on to the royal road to promotion, but he either could not or would not return to the main stream of secular and ecclesiastical business. For the last twenty years of his life, until his death in 1212, he was on the edge of public affairs; his interests became more theological and his friends more narrowly ecclesiastical; he fell under the influence of Cistercian writers and increasingly reflected their ways of thought, as he had reflected those of many others. He never became a peaceable man, and he made an appalling fuss about the slights and set-backs which happen to most men now and then. But his feet were set in more tranquil paths, and he fulfilled in part the promise he had made to the king's clerks:

I am now well stricken in years, and as Job said "My wrinkles bear witness against me" and again "When a few years are come, then shall I go the way whence I shall not return." I shall think over the time I have lost, in the bitterness of my soul, and I shall offer up the residue of my years to my studies and to peace. Farewell my colleagues and my friends. . . .

It was during this "time he had lost" that he had made himself one of the most widely read authors of the twelfth century. Indeed his success as a writer is intimately connected with his position in the world, for it was this which gave him an audience and provided his subject matter. The world knew him as a letter writer, and it read his letters because they were learned without being dead. Without losing anything of the correctness of form demanded by the literary conventions of the day, he made his letters an instrument for conveying moral, legal and theological instruction, and for satire on men and institutions which was one of the passions of his highly sophisticated generation. In his letters he gave to small matters the flavour of the wide world of scholarship.

People like to learn in informal ways and letters are one of the most agreeable forms of instruction that has ever been devised. Letters solved the problem of conveying to a large public some of the results painfully arrived at in the schools. But besides this, they had a practical value. Everyone who wanted to be an administrator needed to know how to write letters. With their passion for reducing everything to a system, the twelfth-century scholars had evolved elaborate rules for letter-writing which were gaining precision when Peter began his career. In the end, this precision killed the art, and Peter of Blois was almost the last of the letter writers before the fourteenth century whose letters could be read for pleasure and

instruction by cultivated readers. Their
success was enormous, and gathered
strength in the fourteenth and fifteenth
centuries. The humanists of the Renaissance found something to criticize in
their form, but they read them, copied
them and indexed them. They were
printed before the end of the fifteenth
century and it was only in the seventeenth century that they ceased to be
part of the living literature of Europe.

This lasting success for a work which
was neither a text-book for the schools,
nor a religious book, is something of
great significance. It indicates the arrival
of a new taste. The secret of Peter of
Blois's success as an author was the same
as the secret of Fulbert's success as a
teacher. They both spoke to their own
age in language, and about things, which
it could understand. If Fulbert spoke to
a handful of scholars and was almost forgotten a hundred years after his death,
while Peter had a large public which
lasted for four hundred years, the reason
lies not in their intrinsic merits but in

the difference between their two ages.
The period occupied by Peter's lifetime
was a time when it was at last possible
to write really popular works. In part
. . . this was due to that mastery of
the past which produced such works
as Gratian's *Decretum* or Peter Lombard's *Sentences.*[2] On these foundations
a new structure of learning could be
built. But in the arts, and in literature,
the second half of the twelfth century
has a different importance. Here also the
task of assimilation had gone on; here
also men had encompassed, and now
commanded their past. But in the process
of absorption they had been overtaken
by a creative spirit, which was not derived from the past, though it was nourished by a medley of influences both
past and present.

[2] Gratian's *Decretum* was fundamental for the
study of canon law. The *Sentences* of Peter
Lombard (*ca.* 1100–*ca.* 1160) became the standard
theological textbook of the Middle Ages. In the
thirteenth century one of the requirements for
the master of theology degree was to write a
commentary on the *Sentences.*—Ed.

JEAN LECLERCQ (b. 1911), a Benedictine
monk and well-known historian, is a leading
authority on the history of monasticism, especially
in the eleventh and twelfth centuries. He is
currently directing a new edition of the works
of St. Bernard. His unusual empathy for his
subject revealed in these studies of monastic
culture helps to explain his emphasis upon the
influence of the monastic liturgy, the framework of
monastic life, in producing an identifiable
monastic culture that was the means by which much
of ancient literary humanism was absorbed in
the Middle Ages. By examining cultural
developments within the monasteries, he calls
attention to a facet of the twelfth-century
renaissance not usually considered. Although he
presents the thesis that a distinct monastic
culture reached its peak in the twelfth century, he
stresses its connection with antiquity by means of the
educational practices within the monasteries and
by ancient learning transmitted through the
writings of the Church Fathers.*

Monastic Culture as a Link
with Antiquity

From the survey of patristic sources[1]
of medieval monastic culture . . . two
conclusions may be drawn. The first is
that there is real continuity between the
patristic age and the medieval monastic
centuries, and between patristic culture
and medieval culture. The monks knew

and loved the patristic writings whose
literary quality they appreciated—the
study of grammar is responsible for
this—and whose religious significance
satisfied the desire for God which monastic life fostered: that is eschatology's
contribution. Nor is their knowledge of
Fathers just bookish learning, limited
to the realm of erudition. The part
played by what can be called the living tradition in the continuity linking Western monasticism to the past
of the whole Church must not be under-

[1] The writings of the Church Fathers. Among
the Latin Church Fathers, St. Jerome (ca. 347–
420) and St. Augustine (354–430) were the most
influential. The patristic age can be considered
as ending with the death of the latter, although
Pope Gregory I (d. 604) is often considered as
one of the church fathers.—Ed.

---

* From Jean Leclercq, *The Love of Learning and the Desire for God*, translated by Catharine
Misrahi (New York: Fordham University Press, 1961), pp. 135–145, 169–171, 180–184. Footnotes
omitted.

estimated. It is often affirmed that monasticism maintained tradition by copying, reading and explaining the works of the Fathers, and that is correct; but it did so also through *living* by what these books contained. This might be called an experiential mode of transmission. Well into the middle of the twelfth century, in the midst of the flowering of scholastic theology, while minds were incurring the risk of getting lost in side issues, the abbeys remained conservatories, as it were, of the great Christian ideas, thanks to the practice of the cult and the diligent reading of the Fathers of the Church. As for the monastic tradition, properly speaking, it can be claimed that . . . there had been no interruption. An evolution had taken place but there was no break, and this continuity found expression in a language profoundly marked by the language of the Fathers.

And—this is a second conclusion—it is this continuity which gives medieval monastic culture its specific character: it is a patristic culture, the prolongation of patristic culture in another age and in another civilization. From this point of view, it seems possible to distinguish, from the eighth to the twelfth century in the West something like two Middle Ages. The monastic Middle Ages, while profoundly Western and profoundly Latin, seems closer to the East than to the other, the scholastic Middle Ages which flourished at the same time and on the same soil. Our intention here is by no means to deny that scholasticism represents a legitimate evolution and a real progress in Christian thought, but rather to point out this coexistence of two Middle Ages. To be sure, the culture developed in the monastic Middle Ages differs from that developed in scholastic circles. The monastic Middle Ages

is essentially patristic because it is thoroughly penetrated by ancient sources and, under their influence, centered on the great realities which are at the very heart of Christianity and give it its life. It is not dispersed in the occasionally secondary problems which are discussed in the schools. Above all, it is based on biblical interpretation similar to the Fathers' and, like theirs, founded on reminiscence, the spontaneous recall of texts taken from Scripture itself with all the consequences which follow from this procedure, notably the use of allegory.

All this is not to say that the monastic Middle Ages is not medieval or that it added nothing to patristic culture. To this assimilation of the Church's past, the monks brought the psychological traits proper to their own time. But the foundations, sources and the general atmosphere in which their culture grew, were patristic. By prolonging patristic culture in a period different from that of the Fathers, they produced a new, and original, yet traditional culture deeply rooted in the culture of the first centuries of Christianity.

Thus while St. Bernard[2] exemplified the "new sensitivity" of the eleventh and twelfth centuries, and has been called "the first of the great French prose writers," he was equally the "last of the Fathers." In fact His Holiness Pius XII proclaimed him as had the humanists of the sixteenth and seventeenth centuries: *ultimus inter patres, sed primis certe non impar* [last among the Fathers, but certainly not inferior to the first]. For this reason, St. Bernard is the symbol of a whole spiritual world, a whole literature which is a prolongation of the pa-

---

[2] St. Bernard (1091–1153) as abbot of Clairvaux became a second founder of the Cistercian Order and did much to spread this strict form of monasticism.—Ed.

tristic age. Dom Morin very correctly perceived that the patristic age had lasted until the twelfth century when he said that a certain anonymous author of that period was the representative of "patristic literature at its decline." In this case, the word decline implies the terminal point of a period; there is nothing pejorative in its meaning since St. Bernard, who belongs to the same period, is not inferior to the ancient Fathers: *Primis certe non impar.* Dom Rousseau has recently shown that, with some new additions and also with some impoverishment, monasticism has, on the whole, faithfully transmitted the values of the patristic age to the medieval Church. In doing so it was not serving the interests of archaeology nor was it motivated by any devotion to the past as such. For one thing, this turning to the sources of ancient culture had about it nothing artificial or constrained; it was free and spontaneous; it was not even done consciously except in cases where circumstances obliged the monks to confront scholastic culture. For another, the past was considered not as being definitely over but as a living reality which continued to animate the present. To attune themselves to it is a spontaneous and, so to speak, vital reaction in monastic circles. It is their life itself, since that life is oriented toward the contemplation of the great mysteries of salvation, and is completely imbued with an intense desire for God which sustains in them the need to recover, through and beyond literary sources the "ancient fervor," the real source of their Christian life, to get as close as possible to the sources of Christianity, to the apostolic age, to the person of our Lord. It is through fidelity to their vocation that the monks, throughout the scholastic period, maintained the patristic spirit.

Third in importance among the sources of medieval monastic culture[3] is classical culture, the word "classical" having in this instance a meaning which requires definition but which, in general acceptance, can be taken to mean the cultural values of pagan antiquity. From the standpoint of the relative worth of its contribution, this source is last in order of importance. But it must be studied; first, because it really does constitute a source, and furthermore because it creates a problem for medievalists and sometimes for readers of the medievalists, as well as for readers of the texts that emanated from medieval monasticism. This problem arises from the diversity of conclusions drawn by historians of medieval literature, a diversity bearing on two issues. On the one hand, as to the knowledge of classical antiquity that the monks actually had: according to some, they were permeated with it; according to others, they possessed merely a superficial acquaintance with it. They knew scarcely more than a few commonplaces, kinds of proverbs or all-purpose quotations such as are found today in the pages of a dictionary. On the other hand, historians are also divided as to how the monks judged the classical authors. According to some, they held them in high esteem, finding in them their masters and their favorite models; according to others, they felt for them only aversion.

What causes this divergence of opinion? First of all it is the general difficulty of finding out what medieval men thought. They scarcely ever spoke of themselves or of what they were doing. They were engaged in living, satisfied to

[3] Leclercq places the Bible and writings of the Church Fathers as first and second in order of importance for their influence upon monastic culture.—Ed.

exist and act without telling us why. Theirs was not a time like ours when books are written on contemporary tendencies. These tendencies did exist but they were translated into action, and it is only the final product which has reached us. This factual evidence allows us at least to pose the psychological problems for which solutions had to be found.

Further, the difficulty is only increased by the very complexity of a problem for which the sources furnish contradictory, or apparently contradictory information. On the one hand, the medieval monks are acquainted with the classics and they use them: that is an undeniable fact. On the other, it often happens that they speak disparagingly of them and advise against reading them. Thus, Alcuin[4] reproaches one of his monastic friends for too great a liking for Virgil and does so by quoting him a verse from the Aeneid, and his own writings are full of Virgilian reminiscences. St. Bernard himself, in order to suppress vain learning, was to call on Persius [A.D. 34–62] as an authority. Such findings would seem to justify the clever remark which has it that Virgil and the other poets were "the enthusiasm of some, the scandal of others, and everybody's concern." Thus the divergent opinions of historians are founded on partial information, each of them based on but a part of the texts and the facts; whereas, in reality, there are two tendencies and two attitudes seemingly contradictory, but which were reconciled: the use of the classics and a distrust for them.

How can this problem be resolved? There can be no question of passing judgment on the monastic Middle Ages. To do this with fairness would require

finding an absolute norm to compare it with, a sort of Golden Age representing perfection. We can perhaps try to ascertain its relative position. Our task will be to establish the facts as objectively as possible and then to try to understand them. The method which seems most likely to insure some degree of success is to examine first the origin of the classical culture of monks, and then its results. . . .

As to the genesis of classical culture in medieval monasticism two questions are seen to arise: when, that is to say, at what time in their lives, did the monks read these authors and what method was used?

Certain monks read the classics, more or less all through their monastic life itself. But all, or almost all had worked on them in school in their youth at the age when memorizing is easy. It is a fact that the classical authors were studied in the cloister schools as well as in the others; even more, as we shall see, than in the others. We have two kinds of proofs for this. First, the existence itself of classical manuscripts which have come down to us. . . . But we possess a still more explicit proof, one which is valid even for manuscripts which have not been preserved; it is found in the catalogues of medieval monastic libraries. A great number of names of classical authors appear in them and this new source furnishes the first precise item of information: these *auctores* are listed generally in the catalogue of the cloister school, not in the catalogue of the community. They are placed not amongst the *libri divini* [religious books], but with the *libri liberales* [liberal books], or even *saeculares* [secular], or, most frequently, *scholastici* [textbooks]; they are school books, classbooks, and, in the sense we continue to use, they are really "classics."

---

[4] Alcuin (735–804) headed the Palace School of Charlemagne and was a leading Carolingian scholar.—Ed.

They appear less frequently in the catalogues of the Cistercian abbeys because they did not have schools; but the *auctores* are nonetheless represented in their writings: the Cistercians had become familiar with them before entering the monastery. No doubt the evolution which monasticism had undergone in the course of its long medieval history must also be taken into account, and necessary distinctions must be made. In the Merovingian period, in many regions, *grammatica* [grammar] was learned in a fairly rudimentary fashion through the use of the psalter alone, but very soon, in the England of the seventh and eighth centuries, the classical authors resumed their role. And from the pedagogical renaissance of the eighth and ninth centuries on, they never again lost it: they were considered as the best models for the learning of Latin.

Who are these *auctores*? They are not just the "classics" in the sense given to this word by today's literary history, that is to say, the authors of the Latin Golden Age. For to the latter were added later writers who were equally considered as authorities on Latinity. . . . Accordingly, attention has been drawn to the fact that while it may be permissible to speak of a "Twelfth-century humanism" no case at all can be made for a "Twelfth-century classicism." In brief, the *scholastici* are *all the ancient authors* who can serve as guides to good expression, the first step in good thinking. To these are joined philosophers, particularly in circles where dialectics plays a greater role than it does in monasticism. Several masters of language, moreover, are masters of reflection as well, like Seneca[5] and Cicero.

Depending on the time and the place, the influence of one schoolman or another, preference was given to one author rather than another. Certain historians of medieval literature have spoken of an *Aetas ovidiana, horatiana* or *virgiliana* [Age of Ovid, Horace or Virgil]; but nothing must be oversimplified and today these too sharply defined classifications have been abandoned.

All future monks benefited by this teaching founded on the authors but each student derived more or less benefit, each master performed his task more or less effectively. Furthermore, in the Middle Ages the word school embraces a wider range of meaning than in our times. The schools were then, no doubt, places where an elementary, then later, secondary education was given to young men of all classes; the program of the *trivium* [grammar, rhetoric, and dialectic] and *quadrivium* [arithmetic, geometry, astronomy, and music] included different series of lessons, that is classes and courses. But the master was far more than a teacher: he was able to pick out the most talented or the most willing workers in the study-group and train them with particular care. This system of selection and specialization favored the rise of a few men of outstanding personality who, in turn, exercised an enriching influence on the environment from which they had come and on a few select disciples. . . .

How were these authors studied, and what procedures were used? By what channels did they penetrate medieval monastic psychology? There were three principal ways: the introduction to the authors, commentary or explanation of the texts, and lastly, copying. No author was taken up without preparation. This introduction was effected through pre-

[5] Seneca (*ca.* 4 B.C.–A.D. 65) was a philosopher and dramatist whose counsel was a restraining influence upon the emperor Nero during the early years of his reign.—Ed.

paratory notes on each which were called *accessus ad auctores* [approach to authors]. There are many examples of this genre extant dating from the twelfth century, but they derive from an older tradition. . . . The first is an anonymous collection, and of the three manuscripts which have preserved it, we know the origin of two. They come from the Benedictine abbey of Tegernsee. As for the other, it is the work of Conrad, a monk of the abbey of Hirsau which, under the abbot William, in 1079 had adopted the Cluniac reform. Conrad, William's pupil, was a schoolmaster at this monastery and wrote, in connection with his teaching, a *Dialogue on the Authors* in which the details of the *accessus* are presented in the form of a conversation between a teacher and his pupil. The *accessus* is a short literary history which takes up for each author the following questions: the life of the author, title of the work, the writer's intention, the subject of the book, the usefulness of its contents and, finally, the question as to what branch of philosophy it belongs to. This whole procedure which was used by the lawyers (both the Canonists and the civilians), theologians, rhetoricians and philosophers, seems to stem from a much more elaborate technique for commentaries on the works of Aristotle. In scholasticism, it was also applied to Holy Scripture; it is practically the same as the one used by Peter Lombard [1140–1160] in the prologue to his commentary on St. Paul. But the underlying intention which inspires these texts is patristic in origin. St. Jerome [*ca.* 347–420], who did not follow the system of the *accessus* in his Prologues to the different books of the Bible, had, however, shaped the direction it was to follow by framing and applying the two postulates on which all this literature rests: opti-

mism with regard to the pagan authors[6] and the necessity of giving them an allegorical interpretation. . . .

One might legitimately suggest that we might admit that the medieval monks were indebted to their classical formation for artistic themes and literary reminiscences and methods, but, in reality, was not all that merely an arsenal of images and quotations which could serve as embellishments, confirmations and modes of expression but which made no profound impression on their own souls? Or, did familiarity with the classics indeed deeply influence the psychology and the personality of the medieval monks? This problem is none other than the problem of the monks' humanism. It is a very delicate one and must first be properly formulated. The question in reality is: do the monks owe to classical tradition, values which are specifically human, with the power to enrich not only their style and intellectual capital, but also their very being?

This question may be answered if we are permitted to make a distinction. If humanism consists in studying the classics for their own sake, in focusing interest on the type of ancient humanity whose message they transmit, then the medieval monks are not humanists. But if humanism is the study of the classics for the reader's personal good, to enable him to enrich his personality, they are in the fullest sense, humanists. As has been said, they had in view a useful and personal end: their education. And what, in fact, did they get from the classics? They took the best these authors had to give. Through contact with them, like all who study the humanities in any

[6] Leclercq defines this optimism as "thinking that everything true or good or simply beautiful that was said, even by pagans, belongs to the Christians."—Ed.

period, they developed and refined their own human faculties. To begin with, they owed to the classics a certain appreciation of the beautiful; this can be seen in the choice the monks made of texts to be preserved and in the quality of the texts they wrote under this influence. In fact, the relative numbers of manuscripts in the libraries show what criterion was used in assessing the authors and the reason why they were read and used. This criterion is their beauty itself. It is because of this taste for the beautiful that Virgil or, depending on the period, Ovid and Horace were preferred to minor writers. The medieval monks were neither antiquarians nor bibliophiles, theirs was in no sense a collector's mentality; they were looking for the useful. They were not pedants nor were they esthetes but they did live intensely. On the one hand, the liturgy developed their feeling for beauty; on the other, asceticism and the cloistered life forbade the pleasures of the senses either crude or refined. Consequently they delighted in beautiful language and beautiful poetry. Certainly they never kept any text which had not charmed them with its beauty. If they read and copied Ovid, for example, it is because his poetry is admirable. At times they drew moral lessons from these authors, but they were not, thanks be to God, reduced to looking to them for that. Their desire was for the joys of the spirit and they neglected none that these authors had to offer. So, if they transcribed classical texts it is simply because they loved them. They loved the authors of the past, not simply because they belonged to the past but because they were beautiful, with a beauty which defies time. Their culture has always been timeless—and it is for that reason that it was effectual.

This familiarity with well chosen models explains the monks' intense need for literary expression and this has been demonstrated in numerous works. No doubt these texts are uneven in quality; still, they are more numerous than is supposed and several remain to be published. Some second-rank authors have left us their names which no longer have any meaning for us; other writings are anonymous. All these texts imply the existence of teachers, a tradition, and an educated public capable of appreciating them and for which they were copied. They reveal the average cultural level of the monastic milieus. . . .

As the time comes for drawing conclusions as to the sources of monastic culture, it is important not to neglect certain nuances in the interests of brevity. The influence of the classical tradition on the monastic culture of the Middle Ages should be neither minimized nor unduly exaggerated. Nothing must be oversimplified or excessively generalized. At every period, from the eighth to the twelfth century, the monks received the education given children in the schools of their times. And almost everywhere and almost always, it was based largely on classical culture. The monks were not obliged either to reject or to further this culture. They assimilated it in different ways, but in every milieu, they welcomed it. Consequently, it would be a distortion of history to draw a distinction between a "monasticism of worship" (*Kultmönchtum*) supposedly that of Cluny, Fleury and other French monasteries and a "monasticism of culture" (*Kulturmönchtum*) presumably that of the countries of the Empire, on the pretext that, from the eleventh century on, Cluny chose not to have in the monastery itself any other school but one for the formation of its own monks. But, there is no need to insist here, on the weakness of such misconceptions.

In order to avoid attributing to classical sources either too great or too small an influence as a component of monastic culture, we must situate them in their relative position among all of the sources which nourish this culture. They are not the only nor the most important component, but they are nonetheless a very real one, and, in conjunction with the others, they contributed to the development of a homogeneous culture. Its foundation was Christian, it was based on Holy Scripture and this was apparent in the domain of thought and imagination as well as in verbal expression. Monastic language is, first of all, a biblical language, entirely fashioned by the Vulgate.[7] Monastic culture was also based on patristics, as is revealed in the topics for reflection, in the allegorical method of exegesis, in the vocabulary and even more so, in the general "style" of literary works. But this fundamentally Christian culture avails itself, in the realm of expression as well as in the realm of the inner life, of antiquity's human experiences—but only of the most beautiful, or of those which it took it upon itself to embellish. From this blend of various influences was born an original culture which was neither purely and simply the culture of the patristic age nor a neo-classical culture after the manner of certain humanists of the fifteenth and sixteenth centuries. The relative proportions of its component elements varied with the environment and the individuals concerned. But, on the whole, this blending confers on monastic culture its own particular quality which grows more and more marked as the twelfth century approaches. Just as ancient monasticism

[7] St. Jerome's Latin translation of the Bible. —Ed.

gave birth to a vocabulary and a language, so, in turn, does medieval monasticism; and insofar as it remains faithful to ancient monasticism, it preserves its language. But it enriches it with elements which come from classical tradition; the latter continues to enter more and more fully into the fabric woven by the Bible and the Fathers, and all these threads are inextricably interwoven in the new sensibility of medieval men. This results in a continuously increasing variety of patterns worked on a changeless background, whose color is monasticism's own. The Carolingian period had been rather a bookish return to ancient sources; in the eleventh and twelfth centuries culture becomes increasingly personal and creative, producing original work without the Carolingian legacy having disappeared: it too had been assimilated in its turn.

This culture does, however, remain profoundly impregnated by literature. It is more literary than speculative. This characteristic differentiates monastic humanism from another, different but no less legitimate, known as scholastic humanism. In the schools, one of the seven liberal arts, dialectics, tends to take precedence over the others to the detriment of grammar, music and rhetoric; clarity of thought was more sought after than artistry in expression and this preoccupation is reflected in a language which, by contrast, allows us all the better to appreciate the nature of a nonscholastic language, that of monasticism. Stripped of ornamentation and abstract, the scholastic language accepts words originating in a sort of unaesthetic jargon, provided only that they be specific. Under these conditions, as has been observed, "the language of orators and poets gives place to that of metaphysicians and logicians. . . . Certain pages of Abailard might have come from the facile pen of one of our classic rationalists, when compared with the warm but very carefully formed effusions of St. Bernard." Instead of assimilating the inheritance from tradition as the monks do, and turning spontaneously toward the past, scholastic milieus are oriented toward the investigation of new problems and the search for new solutions. Clarity, rather than experience or mystery, is their concern and it is attained through the "distinctions." No doubt the monks have no monopoly on grammar, any more than the scholastics have on dialectics; but in the two different milieus the accent falls on different disciplines.

On the other hand, through all it owes to sources which are properly Christian —biblical and patristic—monastic culture differs from still another contemporary form of humanism: the humanism of purely literary writers like Hildebert, Marbod, Peter of Blois, worldly clerics, to say nothing of the Goliards. These stylists easily become precious. Their linguistic artifices very often are not placed at the service of any spiritual message or Christian instruction. However, they do also occasionally produce masterpieces. One of the best representatives of this classic humanism is John of Salisbury, so full of Petronius [d. A.D. 66] and Horace [65–8 B.C.]— to whom "he refers constantly"—and other secular authors. Belonging neither to scholasticism nor to monasticism, this observer who had friends in both milieus saw their distinguishing traits very clearly and he was able to keep his affection for St. Bernard as well as for Gilbert de la Porrée.[8] His letters were not widely disseminated; there are very few manu-

scripts of them in existence. They are, however, very beautiful, as are other writings of the same type.

Monastic style keeps equally distant from the clear but graceless style of the scholastic *quaestiones*[9] and the neo-classic style of these humanists. St. Bernard was able to achieve with perfection the synthesis of all the elements transmitted by the cultural tradition of the West while still according predominance to the Christian content. . . . In this sense, one can rightly speak, with regard to the most representative types of monastic culture . . . of a "monastic style." The literary heritage of all of antiquity, secular and patristic, can be found in it, yet less under the form of imitation or reminiscences of ancient authors than in a certain resonance which discloses a familiarity, acquired by long association, with their literary practices. Much of the wealth of classical tradition had been handed down, already assimilated, in the writings of the Fathers. Let us reflect, for example, on all that the *De officiis* of St. Ambrose [*ca.* 340–397] or St. Jerome's letters owed to Cicero. This was both a way of thinking and a way of expressing oneself. Thus the *lectio divina* [religious reading] complemented harmoniously the grammar that was learned in school. And when the monks wrote, their literary technique showed no "bookish" traits. Their imitation of literary models became spontaneous and for that very reason, often scarcely discernible. Under these conditions, grammar was no obstacle to the longing for heaven; literature was not a screen between the soul and its God but rather, it was transcended. The purpose of liberal studies

---

8 Gilbert de la Porrée (1076–1154), a great teacher at Chartres and Paris, was important for his writings on logic and metaphysics, including the first systematic attempt to explain God by principles drawn from metaphysics.—Ed.

9 The questions, or problems, used as a point of departure by scholastic writers in their formal presentations whereby they gave authorities and arguments on both sides of a subject and then presented a reconciliation of opposed views. —Ed.

had been attained. The most dangerous author had been "converted," and in the very mind of the student of literature. Learned once and then forgotten, perhaps even denied, they remained present in the deepest recesses of the soul. The monastic humanists are not like those of the Renaissance, torn between two cultures. They are not partially pagan. They are wholly Christian, and in that sense, are in possession of the *sancta simplicitas* [holy simplicity].

In 1950, forty-six years after the meeting addressed by Munro, the American Historical Association again held a session devoted to the twelfth-century renaissance. This sustained scholarly interest testifies both to the importance of the subject and to the unresolved differences in interpretation of the period. EVA MATTHEWS SANFORD (1894–1954) provided a synthesis of scholarly opinion after nearly a half century of research and gave her own interpretation of the twelfth-century renaissance. It was her view that the conviction of continuity with the ancient world found in the histories written in the Middle Ages was a distinguishing characteristic of the twelfth century—a conviction that prevented men of that time from seeing any break between themselves and antiquity. Miss Sanford taught both ancient and medieval history at Sweet Briar College, and her published works show this dual interest. They include *The Mediterranean World in Ancient Times* (1938), a translation of the fifth-century writer Salvianus (1930), and an an article on "The Study of Ancient History in the Middle Ages (1944)."*

History as a Continuous Thread

There are two phases of our problem: what do we mean by a renaissance, and does the twelfth century conform to this definition sufficiently to justify giving it the name? Since the term was first applied to the humanism of the Italian *Quattrocento* and to the appropriation of the antique in combination with direct observation of man and nature in its art, its original connotations were in the fields of classical scholarship and of literature and art. The humanists' reaction against their own concept of mediaevalism, as a period of dull stagnation dominated by blind acceptance of authority, and limited by indifference to the material world, gave rise to the idea of "rebirth" or *renaissance*, and to Michelet's classic phrase, "the rediscovery of the world and of man." Few scholars would now insist on the literal meaning of the word "renaissance," with its

* From Eva Matthews Sanford, "The Twelfth Century—Renaissance or Proto-Renaissance?" Reprinted by permission from *Speculum*, XXVI (1951) published by The Mediaeval Academy of America, pp. 635–641. Footnotes omitted.

suggestion of a preceding state of coma, if not of actual death. . . . If we substitute the criterion of intensified interest and vitality for rebirth and rediscovery, we still have to reckon with the Renaissance factors of individualism, secularism, skeptical criticism of traditional authority, and the creation of new standards and techniques in scholarship, literature and the arts, based in part on the interworking of classical and contemporary factors. We have also to consider the conspicuous influence on humanistic scholars and artists, and on Renaissance thought in general, of the "notion of belonging to a new time" and of the historical definition of the Renaissance as the transition from the mediaeval to the modern world.

In a recent paper Professor Wallace Ferguson has discussed our need of a new synthesis of the Renaissance as "an age of moral, religious, intellectual and aesthetic crisis, closely interrelated with acute economic, political and social crisis." He considers the revival of antiquity as a great, but secondary, causative force in this age. He notes decisive changes in all countries of western Europe from the beginning of the fourteenth century, and therefore proposes that the Renaissance, as the transition from mediaeval to modern culture, should be dated from about 1300 to 1600. This proposal embodies a most comprehensive view of the Renaissance. It accents the principle of crisis as a determinant, an extension of the "new age" emphasis, and it reminds us of a chronological problem. If we consider the twelfth century, according to Professor Haskins' chronology, as extending to about 1250, when "the signature of the thirteenth century" became clearly recognizable in literature, art, and thought, the period between a Renais-

sance of the twelfth century and the inauguration of the major Renaissance would be only fifty years long. This may lead us to a fruitful application of the obvious differences between the organic phenomena of the two periods, the one representing the height of mediaeval culture, and the other a decidedly transitional phase, but both contributing directly in their different ways to the emergence of the modern world. . . .

As far as literature and art are concerned, Erwin Panofsky, in his brilliant essay on "Renaissance and Renascences," proposed the terms "proto-humanism" and "proto-Renaissance" for the twelfth century. . . . I find the specific illustrations by which he supports this thesis more convincing in art than in literature. But he brings out an essential difference between the two periods in their attitude toward the classical models that both used so much in their various ways. Writers and artists of the twelfth century did not recognize a cultural break between antiquity and their own time, whereas those of the fifteenth century not only recognized but emphasized it. The distinction between the twelfth century and the later Renaissance in regard to direct stimulus provided for further development, however, does not hold good in all the fields that interest historians.

Professor McIlwain has demonstrated the fallacy of contrasting the political theories and institutions of the twelfth century with those of the Renaissance in this respect. In "Mediaeval Institutions in the Modern World" he wrote: "In the field of political institutions and ideas, I venture to think that what Professor Haskins has termed 'the Renaissance of the Twelfth Century' marks a more fundamental change than the later developments to which we usually attach the word 'Renaissance'; that the constitutionalism of the modern world owes as much, if not even more, to the twelfth and thirteenth centuries than to any later period of comparable length until the seventeenth." He cited especially the mediaeval limitations of governmental authority by private rights, the development of parliamentary institutions, and the gradual assimilation of Roman constitutionalism. The slow process of assimilation of Roman law was speeded up in twelfth-century Italy by the rivalries of empire, papacy, and north Italian communes, which in this period developed the autonomous institutions that contributed so much to their leadership in fifteenth century culture. The University of Bologna and the work of the great glossators[1] show that in the field of Roman law the twelfth and thirteenth centuries left no opportunity for fundamental "discovery" but only for continued study and application of foundations already well and truly laid.

In the field of the natural sciences, we are increasingly aware that the basis for the phenomenal progress of the sixteenth and seventeenth centuries was established before the Renaissance, and that the translations of Greek and Arabic scientific works in the twelfth and thirteenth centuries provided the initial stimulus for such significant research in scientific theory and techniques as that carried on at Padua from about 1300. It is now generally recognized that Roger Bacon [d. 1292], as his own words testify, was not the first mediaeval scholar to set a high value on experimental science, and to formulate sound criteria for it. The net results of mediaeval science, in

[1] Roman law was taught by the addition of explanatory comments to the *Digest* in the form of marginal glosses. Often these glosses outgrew the text itself, but they provided a necessary step for the assimilation of Roman law.—Ed.

comparison with the achievements of the sixteenth century, are small indeed, yet the period of incubation began here rather than in the fifteenth century. In the latter period, although many humanists tended to scorn the natural sciences in favor of classical learning (as some have been known to do even in later times), the careful re-examination of mediaeval scientific works together with those of the Greeks and Romans, and the increasing interchange of ideas and techniques between scholars, artists, and craftsmen, prepared the way more fully for the dynamic scientific achievements of the sixteenth century. It would seem that in the scientific as well as in the political field the twelfth century exerted a sufficiently direct influence on later developments to make its definition as a "proto-Renaissance" untenable.

Unqualified insistence on a twelfth-century Renaissance, however, involves the risk of emphasizing the Renaissance characteristics of the period at the expense of its essentially mediaeval qualities. In many respects, like all periods of dynamic activity, it was an age of transition, but the factors of change, significant though they were, still operated to extend and enrich the traditional pattern of a unified Christian culture, with its closely knit communities and personal ties, rather than to destroy them. There were many crises in the twelfth century, but there was not, it seems to me, the over-all motivation in terms of crisis that Professor Ferguson attributes to the later Renaissance. For all the new phases of economic, political, social, aesthetic and intellectual life in the twelfth century, I have not found in it that prevalent consciousness of a new age, or the determination of ideas by the sense of newness, that is so conspicuous in the fifteenth century.

The conviction of continuity with the ancient world is one controlling factor here. We see it in the "Christian synthesis" of Hebrew, Greek, Hellenistic, and Roman with Christian history, and in the historical pattern of the four empires, ending with the Roman, which was expected to endure till the end of the created world. Mediaeval historians, even those who fully recognized that the imperial power in the west had been transferred from Roman to Frankish and German rulers, often echoed the old statement, "The last age is the Roman, in which we now live." They did not look back to the ideas and achievements of antiquity for fresh inspiration from a distant source, but as a direct inheritance and a native possession. This conviction of the unity of history made them unconscious of anachronism and blocked off many approaches to historical criticism, but it also saved the ancient world from the aspect of unreality that it has had for many students in later ages. With the great increase in historical writing in the twelfth century, the theme of *renovatio* [renewal] appears, as it does also in the political theories of the imperial partisans. Peter of Blois' famous defence of the study of ancient history may serve to illustrate this "Renaissance" attitude, which appears frequently in the works of the chief twelfth-century writers, but, as in this case, within the framework of the mediaeval pattern of world history: "However dogs may bark at me, and pigs grunt, I shall always imitate the writings of the ancients: these shall be my study, nor, while my strength lasts, shall the sun find me idle. We are like dwarfs on the shoulders of giants, by whose grace we see farther than they. Our study of the works of the ancients enables us to give fresh life to their finer ideas, and rescue them from time's oblivion and man's neglect." Here is no blind reverence for ancient authority, but a dignified, though not unmodest assumption that a twelfth-century scholar could and should see farther than the giants of the past. Here, also, is one of many possible answers to the common charge that mediaeval scholars in general feared and distrusted the influence of pagan ideas. The strictures of [St.] Bernard of Clairvaux and other ascetic Christians represent a significant but by no means a universal mediaeval attitude. They were often occasioned by the genuine devotion to classical literature displayed by contemporary humanists. Not only the intimate knowledge that twelfth-century writers exhibit of the works of Vergil, Ovid, Horace, and other Latin authors, but the frequent occurrence, even in theological works, of pagan *exempla virtutis* and the wide range of mediaeval quotations from classical authors, show that the classics were commonly read and used for their own value, and not merely to assail pagan corruption or to despoil the Egyptians. . . .

To those Renaissance historians who broke away from the mediaeval scheme of history, antiquity was an age long past, separated by a thousand years from their own time, and hence studied more objectively, for its possible contributions to their new and rapidly changing world. In the twelfth century, the sense of continuity with the past is conspicuous in the leading cultural centers of northern France, England, the Rhineland and the upper Danube, where the Latin language and literature were not native to the same degree that they were in southern France and Italy. Though Latin was no longer a mother tongue, even in the latter areas, it was in many respects a living language, flexibly handled by educated men, without the artificial restrictions on style and vocabulary that extreme Ciceronians later imposed on it. The hymns and lyric and narrative poems of the twelfth and thirteenth centuries testify that poets found in Latin a natural medium for the expression of their ideas and emotions. The occurrence of both Latin and vernacular versions of the same themes, and the evidences of cross-fertilization between Latin and vernacular literature, deserve serious consideration in this connection. Greek literature, however, remained unknown, aside from the arid and prosaic Latin epitomes of Homer, and such works as had been earlier incorporated in the Latin tradition by the great translators of the Roman period, or by the popular versions of Aesop's fables and the romance of Apollonius of Tyre, for example. The names of Greek authors were known from histories of literature; the scholars who diligently sought out and translated Aristotle's books on logic and natural science might presumably have recovered literary texts also, if they had wished, but they left this important phase of the appropriation of the antique for a later time.

Secularism, individualism, and criticism of established authority are much stressed as distinguishing characteristics of the Renaissance. How far should our appraisal of the twelfth century be influenced by the ecclesiastical character of its culture as contrasted with later secularism? Professor Boyce has wisely pointed out that the terms "secular" and "ecclesiastical" are not mutually exclusive in the Middle Ages. When education was provided chiefly by monastic and cathedral schools, and private tutors were usually monks or priests, when there were few non-clerical careers for intellectual men, and students, however worldly,

could claim benefit of clergy, when all society, except for the small minority of Jews and avowed heretics, was united in one Christian fellowship, there could be no clear line of demarcation between the religious and the secular except that drawn by extremists. Not all priests and bishops, monks and friars were insulated from the world by an ecclesiastical ivory tower. Those whose undue worldliness aroused the righteous indignation of contemporary reformers were sometimes, though not always, among the intellectual leaders of their day, and some very secular works were dedicated to ecclesiastical patrons. The learning and literature of the courts of Henry II, Eleanor of Aquitaine, and the Norman rulers of Sicily remind us that patronage was not entirely clerical, though there were fewer wealthy lay patrons—as, indeed, there were fewer wealthy men—than in the fifteenth century.[2] Professor Thompson and others have taught us that not all the laity were illiterate; the twelfth century saw a marked increase in the reading public, and the desire of the new readers for edification and entertainment from books met with a notable response on the part of both Latin and vernacular writers. . . .

The most notable buildings that afforded opportunity for the development of architecture and the decorative arts were churches, but in their decoration secular motifs were blithely introduced with apparent unconsciousness of incongruity. Though the traditional symbolism of many of these motifs is well established, the naturalism and freshness with which they are often presented makes them no less convincing evidence that details of the physical world were

[2] Henry II, king of England from 1154–1189, and his queen, Eleanor of Aquitaine, were both patrons of learning and literature.—Ed.

recognized as belonging in the religious context. As the church was the unifying factor in society, its interests embraced many secular elements which later ages associate with the body politic and social rather than with the communion of saints. Obviously, however, the ecclesiastical side of the scales was more heavily weighted than the secular, whereas the next few generations were to change the balance. Here there is a fundamental difference between twelfth-century and Renaissance culture, though the contrast is relative rather than absolute.

The question of individualism is also a relative one. We no longer identify outstanding individuals in the Middle Ages as forerunners of the Renaissance, but recognize Abelard, for example, as a natural product of his time, albeit an exceptional one. In what age would Abelard not have been exceptional? The personal tone of much lyric and satirical poetry is pertinent here. Anonymity was not always due to the Christian subordination of individual claims to creative talent in favor of the Creator. Sometimes, it was expressly attributed to fear of malicious opponents, and sometimes, as in the case of the most popular treatise on education, the Pseudo-Boethius, *De disciplina scholarium*, to the desire to gain a wider public by fathering one's book on a noted ancient authority.[3] Again there is a marked difference in proportion between the two periods; individualism is by no means exceptional in the twelfth century, but it runs rampant in the fifteenth.

Outspoken criticism of traditional authority was not unknown in the twelfth

[3] Boethius (d. 524) translated two of Aristotle's logical treatises into Latin. These were the only parts of Aristotle available in the West until the twelfth century. His own work, *The Consolation of Philosophy*, was very popular throughout the Middle Ages.—Ed.

century, when the range of ecclesiastical questions open to dispute was somewhat wider than it was on the eve of the Reformation. The risk of a trial for heresy was not always a deterrent to scholars convinced of their own sound judgment. Skepticism and the spirit of objective inquiry did not always provoke condemnation, and Abelard's critical method survived numerous attacks before his works were incorporated in the curriculum of the University of Paris. His rational thesis, "By doubting we are led to inquire, and by inquiry we perceive the truth," represents the constructive theological approach of the period better than the attacks it provoked from the more intellectually inert of his contemporaries. . . .

For the Age of Faith assumed the exercise of reason, within the bounds of its clearly defined and finite world, which still provided ample range for speculative and critical thought. In his memorable Harvard Tercentenary lecture on Mediaeval Universalism, Etienne Gilson pointed out the intellectual obligations imposed by the mediaeval conviction of universal truth as valid for all men at all times and places. In the twelfth century a unified society with a common meaning for all its members still transcended local differences; its culture was still non-national and non-racial, though there was an increasing consciousness of local and national distinctions. Changes were being wrought by the expansion of commerce and industry with their new contacts, implements and techniques, and their new types of communities and opportunities. Many political and social adjustments were required by these changes and by the concomitant increase in population and production. In their later stages these changes were to create a new world and in so doing, break down the unity of the old, but they had not as yet destroyed the equilibrium.

As we look back at the twelfth century, it is difficult to remember that feudal and agrarian institutions were still actively developing, with more conscious definition of their functions and principles than before, and were still being furthered rather than weakened by the expanding horizons of the age.

To sum up: the designation of the twelfth century as a proto-Renaissance seems both misleading and inadequate. But if we describe it, without considerable qualifications, as a Renaissance period, do we not risk underestimating and even distorting its real character? Can we use this term without implying more identity than the twelfth century really had with the later Renaissance, with its atmosphere of crisis and its consciousness of a new age, in which the secular motivation of political, social, economic, and intellectual life replaced the universalism that still directed and inspired the thought and action of the twelfth century? I must confess that I have found the idea of a twelfth-century Renaissance very useful in teaching undergraduates mediaeval history, and I had not really questioned its validity before I wrote this paper. Now I am not so sure. If the men of the Renaissance had not put mediaevalists on the defensive by insistence on their rescue of the world and man from mediaeval ignorance and oblivion, should we feel the need of defining the earlier period as a renaissance? Should we not rather be satisfied to let the twelfth century stand on its own merits as a dynamic period of mediaeval culture, which made fruitful contributions to the development of modern man and the modern world without forfeiting its own essentially mediaeval character?

Historians of art and architecture especially
have been confronted with the problem posed
by medieval artists using classical objects, art
forms, and even subject matter. In spite of the
obvious continuity with antiquity, the artists who
placed these classical models in the setting of
the twelfth century consciously and unconsciously
transformed the classical materials. WILLIAM S.
HECKSCHER (b. 1904) brings the findings
of other art historians to bear upon the special
case of medieval re-use of ancient gems and examines
the patterns of thought that permitted both
continuity and adaptation of these objects from
antiquity. His conclusions, in agreement with
other studies of twelfth-century art, would suggest
that the intellectual movement of that period
was essentially a new movement with its own
characteristics separating it from other movements
both earlier and later. He has taught art history both
in the United States and at the University of
Utrecht, where he was also director of its
Iconological Institute. His own work in iconology
is exemplified by his book on *Rembrandt's
Anatomy of Dr. Nicolaas Tulp* (1958). On
several occasions he has been a member of the
Institute for Advanced Study at Princeton University,
and he is now Benjamin N. Duke Professor of
Art at Duke University.*

Classical Concepts in a New Setting

The most obvious examples of relics
of Antiquity in mediaeval setting are the
ancient gems and precious stones which,
in spite of their pagan carvings, were
used by mediaeval craftsmen for the decoration of covers of prayer-books, crozi-
ers, crosses, relic-shrines and other ecclesiastical objects; not to mention the personal seals and signet-rings of the highest
dignitaries of the Church. Although the
importance of the subject has frequently
been stressed, it has remained a sort of
"no man's land" between the fields of
Classical Archaeology and Mediaeval
History of Art. There exists, to my
knowledge, no serious attempt to in-

* From William S. Heckscher, "Relics of Pagan Antiquity in Mediaeval Settings," *Journal of
the Warburg Institute*, I (London, 1937–38), pp. 204–220. Footnotes omitted.

terpret this significant chapter of mediaeval aesthetics, which incidentally has some important bearing on the psychology of mediaeval tolerance; for in studying the use of ancient stones in mediaeval jewellery it becomes apparent that orthodox Christianity and pagan Antiquity lived here in peaceful symbiosis.

To relate this event to its general background it will be necessary first to describe in what terms mediaeval Christianity conceived of its own relation to antiquity and what general rules it consequently observed (if any) in the treatment of pagan relics. Secondly, we shall examine the particular concepts of beauty, which dictated or permitted the mediaeval appreciation of ancient gems. In the third place, we shall mention the elements of magic and superstition which entered into this appreciation. And finally, we shall give a number of detailed illustrations, which will show the process by which individual remains of pagan antiquity were incorporated in Christian settings.

In dealing with the first three points it will be neither possible nor desirable to avoid reference to well-known facts and repetition of well-established theories. . . .

A clear-cut idea of Antiquity as a historical period of the past did not exist in the Middle Ages. Mediaeval thinkers were convinced that they themselves were still citizens of the empire which had been founded by Augustus. Though they were eager to assimilate in their historical constructions all available accounts of events from the creation of the world down to their own present, political history to them meant first of all Roman, post-Republican history. This helps to explain the relative ease with which they placed a Christian meaning upon pagan prophecies such as Virgil's "Messianic Eclogue"[1] or reconciled Christian ethics with that of the pagan philosophers. . . .

At first glance it might seem strange that there should be an admission of a fundamental union between Paganism and Christianity; for it is generally assumed that the sympathy with these ideas represents but a small undercurrent of thought and was confined to a few "mediaeval humanists" whose endeavour it was to extol the values of the pagan era—values which could only be reached by the pathways of heresy. The idea of concordance, however, was quite common and anything but heretical, as it went in the wake of dogmatic tenets held by the Church. To show this, it will suffice to refer to the mediaeval idea of a "final realm" in which all earthly occurrence was thought to be consummated. This final realm, called the "Fourth Monarchy" in St. Jerome's Commentary on Daniel and depicted by St. Augustine as the "City of God" on earth, was expected to last until the arrival of the Antichrist; that is, until the end of the world and up to the preliminaries of the Last Judgment. Politically speaking, the Fourth Monarchy was supposed to be embodied in the Roman Empire. The Empire had been founded by Caesar Augustus, the prince who had brought peace to the world in that he put an end to the civil wars. It was Christ's birth that had simultaneously given spiritual peace to "all men of good will." This formula, essentially Augustinian, still rings in Beatrice's promise to Dante:

[1] The fourth Eclogue of the Roman poet Virgil written about 40 B.C. foretold the birth of a deliverer from the world's sufferings. Medieval Christian writers mistakenly identified the expected child with Christ.—Ed.

E sarai meco senza fine cive
Di quella Roma onde Christo
è Romano.[2]

Even in the elaborate writings of the later Middle Ages all 'historical' constructions (by men like Otto of Freising) were meant to support the one dominating idea of unity, the *principium unitatis* [principle of unity] as it was called.

It is in the light of this "*principium unitatis*" that we must understand the mediaeval attempts to restore Antiquity which go under the name of *renovatio* [renewal]. No doubt these attempts continue during the Renaissance and later, but the predominant attitude changes. Petrarch [1304–1374] was perhaps the first to become aware of Antiquity as a "lost paradise" whose ruins and remains became to him venerable (and therefore untouchable) relics of a past which was irrevocably detached from his own epoch. Hence the new conception of an intervening "middle" age; hence the modern view of Antiquity as a self-contained historical period, the products of which can neither be simply restored nor bluntly adapted, but may well serve as models to be emulated or even surpassed. "Imitatio" [imitation] rather than "Renovatio" was the slogan of the Renaissance. But to the mediaeval mind, the cult of the Antique meant not so much a revival of a thing which had died as the removal of obstructions which impaired the maintenance of things extant.

To illustrate this point we may refer to a case of political *renovatio* which affords a good example of an unhampered use of pagan symbols on the part of people who were convinced that Antiquity was still with them.

In 1143 the City of Rome was over-

[2] "And you will be everlastingly a citizen of that Rome whereof Christ is a Roman."—Ed.

taken by an internal crisis which—primarily caused by the example of self-governed towns in the neighbourhood —soon turned into something specifically "Roman." The new government, as a first step, overthrew the aristocratic régime of the city and made itself master of the Capitol. The spokesmen of this popular party made ample use of such literary paraphernalia as were honoured by old Roman usage and tradition. They adopted the title of *Sacer Senatus Populi Romani* [sacred senate of the Roman people]. Their programme was founded on two main principles: They wanted to do away with the Pope's earthly power, thus restoring the *sacerdotium* [priesthood], and they placed their hopes for a secular reform on those who held the *regalis potestas* [regal power] of the fourth monarchy, the emperors of the Roman Empire. It was their duty, they proclaimed, to bring about the necessary *renovatio* in close collaboration with the Senate itself. The addresses by which the Senate and People implored the Emperor over and over again *ut Romam veniat* [to come to Rome] are teeming with *renovatio* terminology.

It seems quite possible that the famous pamphlet called the *Graphia aureae urbis Romae* [Description of the golden city of Rome] was composed in the course of these political endeavours. It would certainly have been a valuable instrument of justification in the hands of a legation to the court of the German Emperor, and, beyond that, a means for propagandist dissemination of the Senate's ideas.

The *Graphia* consists of three books. An introductory *Historia Romana a Noe usque ad Romulum* [Roman History from Noah to Romulus] serves to prove the sacred root of the City, and it seems expressly to be written for the *Graphia*.

The *Historia* is followed by a copy of the *Mirabilia urbis Romae* [Marvels of the City of Rome], which can be defined as an antiquarian catalogue of pagan Rome, i.e. its walls, temples, baths, etc. It had only been issued a few years before as the work of a papal specialist on Roman topography, a Canon Benedictus in all probability. The third book is a learned handbook of the imperial (Byzantine) court ceremonial, the so-called *Libellus de Cerimoniis* [Book of Ceremonies]. The *Libellus*, fantastic as it may seem to the modern reader, was to play an important part in the rites with which some 150 years later Cola di Rienzo celebrated his coronation.[3] In the twelfth century it failed to impress the German Emperors. Konrad III was never crowned, while Frederic Barbarossa declined the alliance repeatedly offered to him by the Senate.

The Roman Senate and the composer of the *Graphia* treated Roman *renovatio* as a matter of reality. There is another example similar in tendency, which, perhaps, entails even more evidence of an intimate approach toward Antiquity. One of the few secular buildings of mediaeval Rome, parts of which have remained unimpaired, is the enigmatic *Casa dei Crescenzi*, a brick tower near Ponte Rotto. Half columns, embedded in its walls (columns that are obvious imitations of antique prototypes), support some well-preserved specimens of antique friezes. The latter are stuck on to the front and the sides of the building without any logical sequence. An inscription in Leonine hexameters states that "Nicolaus, owner of this house, was not incited by vain love of glory, when he built it, but that he did it *Romae veterem renovare decorem* [to renew the

[3] He led a revolution in Rome and set himself up as tribune of the people in 1347.—Ed.

former beauty of Rome]." One could imagine, though this is merely an idle play of thought, that this man Nicolaus, who was neither cleric nor nobleman, had some kind of connexion with the popular party. One of the councillors of the Senate, frequently mentioned in the documents of the party as a member of the delegations which voiced its programmes, is referred to as *Nicholaus socius noster* [our colleague].

In their striving for *renovatio* these revolutionary governors of Rome liked to intersperse and embellish their system of political reform with examples taken from Roman ideology. The man who built the brick tower near Ponte Rotto may have been incited by similar prospects and ideals.

Within this "optimistic" group there must have prevailed a boundless belief in the possibilities of renewal, while of necessity their compass with regard to Antiquity, which they approached with a sense of intimacy, was comparatively narrow. In order to establish a criterion for these relative judgments on "intimacy" and "smallness of scope" we must set in contrast to these politicians the attitude of a man whose outlook upon *renovatio* was tinged by religious eschatology. The greatest conceivable distance, the highest degree of resignation, and at the same time the most sweeping "all-round" view of what Roman and pagan Antiquity may have meant in the Middle Ages, is found in the often discussed *Roma* and *Item de Roma* of the cleric Hildebert of Lavardin (died 1133) who was a pessimist in matters of *renovatio*.

This pessimism, no less than the pragmatic optimism of the politicians, is rooted in the *principium unitatis*. The eventual goal of the mediaeval striving for unity was peace: PAX. It had been brought into existence with the beginnings of the *Romanum Imperium* [Roman Empire]. It had been defined spiritually by St. Augustine as *summum bonum*, the sovereign good, as *tranquillitas ordinis* [tranquillity of order]. Yet it ran permanent dangers through human weakness. The Fourth Monarchy was spoken of as the *aetas debilis* [weak age]. A metaphysical hope was superimposed on its obvious physical decline: *vide regno Christi crescente regnum mundi paulatim imminui*,[4] says Otto of Freising, and the same is proclaimed by Hildebert. He balances his enthusiastic view of Rome's grandeur—*par tibi Roma nihil* [nothing equals Rome]—by a reference to the welfare of the cross (i.e. the approach of the heavenly realm), which, as he puts it, can only be gained through the fall of all earthly splendour. . . . Hildebert makes it clear in the second part of the "Elegy" that Rome's monuments, symbolizing by their deplorable state of dilapidation the irresistible decline of the realm, had ceased to be things, the aspect of which would provoke a desire for *renovatio*. The ancient sites, monuments, and statues, fallen to pieces and deprived of their former decorations, could only be regarded as specimens of "Vanity"—signal examples of divine chastisement.

At the same time, the very greatness of these remnants could not but impress the beholder with his own weakness. "Neither can a structure be erected equal to the wall that stands, nor can one single ruin be restored—*aut restaurari sola ruina potest*. So much has been preserved, so much has been destroyed that it is impossible either to match a portion that still stands upright, or to restore a portion that is ruined."

[4] "Note that as the kingdom of Christ expands the worldly kingdom is constantly diminishing." —Ed.

Two facts emerge from this lament:

(1) In quenching the last sparks of a hope for *renovatio*, Hildebert renounces the actual restoration of the ruins. Under the impact of his conception of Roman grandeur he admits the feebleness of his own times, which he describes as impotent to rescue *Caesaris et superum templa* [temples of Caesar] and to reshape them in their original form.

(2) It is the vision of this original form which arouses his nostalgic feelings. In the very fragments he admires their abstract idea. The fragmentary state as such he does not admire, but laments. Only the Renaissance period came to admire ruins on account of their intrinsic beauty.

If we compare Hildebert's attitude with that of the optimistic reformers, we find that two seemingly contradictory ideas were in common to both parties. Both believed in the "Fourth Monarchy" which implied that they were directly linked with Antiquity. At the same time both had a feeling of distance towards Antiquity which evoked the desire (or despair) of *renovatio*. It is clear that the two ideas are interrelated. They stand in inverse proportion to one another: An increased feeling of distance produces aspects of grandeur which an intimate view does not afford, and *vice versa*. While Hildebert and other men of his group looked upon the architecture and statuary art of the Romans as pathetic reminders of distant grandeur, the *Graphia* and the documents issued by the popular party treated the available remains as useful specimens—intact and dainty, as were the friezes employed in Nicolaus' brick tower.

The mediaeval "humanists," because they lamented the fall of Rome, have often enough been hailed as predecessors of the Renaissance. This is misleading. For it was only with the dawn of new historical theories, when the scholastic thought began to fade, that the idea of distance could become fatal to that of continuity. The new nostalgia was no longer dependent upon the belief in a pre-ordained eschatology, but was nourished by the emotion of historical sentiment, under the spell of which the fall of great cities began to assume the glamour of an individual destiny.

No trace of this "individualism" of fate is found in the mediaeval conception of the goddess Fortuna [Chance] who bridges the gulf between the permanent order of the eternal world and the changing order of the temporal. She was supposed to serve as a "lever" of God's secret intentions and so was held responsible for all features of earthly debility, which she imparted as a blind but righteous instrument of divine Providence. Whatever seemed to be caused by "chance," all kinds of catastrophies that occurred in the human province as well as in that of inanimate things, were held to be the work of Fortuna, who by turning her wheel dispensed good and evil to those in the sphere of her competence. Fortuna's destructive effects bore the distinct character of punishment.

The "classical" description in twelfth-century literature of Fortuna's domain is that of Alanus of Lille in his *Anticlaudianus*. Fortuna's territory reflects the ambiguous character of its mistress: Zephyrus and Boreas meet at its boundary. The pleasing song of the nightingale is heard, but also the ominous call of the owl which foretells disaster. Fruitful trees are intermingled with the barren. Large trees are contrasted with small. A stream of sweetness is endangered by the bitterness of an infernal stream. For-

tuna's mansion stands upon a rock, and its construction reveals the same ambiguity of appearance: while one portion of her palace, radiant with the splendour of silver, gems and gold, crowns the summit of the rock, the other, consisting of squalid material (*vili materie*), is about to tumble down the slope in ruins.

In fictitious descriptions of palaces . . . precious materials played an important part as embodiments of majestic power. Alanus added boldly the image of contrast. The baseness of the material and the dilapidated state in Fortuna's palace indicate that, in a mortal being, the possession of wealth and power can at any moment change into destitution and want. Yet this very antithesis makes it clear that to Alanus and his readers gold and silver and gems, though precarious possessions, represented an adequate symbol of power and glory. Under the temporary reign of Fortuna they appear as the "opposite" of ruins.

We shall see that this seemingly trivial formula supplies a clue for discovering some of the reasons why the mediaeval interest in relics of the Antique was so strongly specialized on gems and stones. What the mediaeval mind chiefly sought in the remains of the past was—in contra-distinction to modern romanticism— the permanent form, the opposite of the ruin.

The flawless appearance of ancient stones, their transparency, their stern resistance to corrosion or *patina*, which secures the permanence of the shape once assigned to them, fully responded to mediaeval ideas of the beautiful. In the mediaeval conception of hierarchies of perfection a complete thing automatically ranks above an incomplete one. To a modern spectator a structure fallen to pieces may reveal a tragic contrast or an idyllic union between the efforts of man and the impersonal forces of nature. The mediaeval view will not allow of such pleasant mingling of opposites. It conceives the universe as a static order in which each thing is well established and ranked, according to the divine plan. Such a system rejects anything that has forsaken the form originally assigned to it. A palace, to the mediaeval mind, is beautiful as a palace; as a ruin it ceases to be so. The various stages of decay can only mean a diminishing and slackening of a once flawless form; but never can they lead up into another stage of existence in which the object concerned might claim a new significance and a beauty of its own. To my knowledge there is in mediaeval literature no collective noun which has the range of our term "ruin."

In the *Distinctiones Dictionum*, the etymological and moralistic dictionary which Alanus of Lille wrote in the second half of the twelfth century, we find under *frangere* in the first place: *proprie dividere signat humiliare unde Prudentius in Psychomachia: frangit Deus omne superbum.*[5] And St. Thomas, in his famous definition of the beautiful postulates that there be: *primo quidem integritas sive perfectio; quae enim diminuta sunt, hoc ipso turpa sunt*—"in the first place integrity or perfection: things impaired are ugly for that very reason."

It is interesting to illustrate these statements by mediaeval representations of architectural destruction. They exemplify the limitations and "short-comings" to which in the Middle Ages the faculty of visualizing (and thus portraying) ruins was doomed. In fact, the only way

by which ruins could be rendered was that of showing the actual occurrence of *frangere*, the breaking asunder of a whole into various pieces; pieces which in their turn formed intact units in themselves . . . for example, the Fall of Babylon as represented in a Beatus manuscript of the Cathedral of Burgo de Osma, dating from the end of the eleventh century. In the upper half of the minature we see people tumbling down and in their fall hanging on to such entire units as columns and arches. The actual outlines of those scattered pieces could be rejoined as if they were pieces of a jig-saw puzzle. In an English thirteenth century miniature of a falling city, the steeple of the central tower looks as if it were a lid turning on hinges.

In a good many cases, even this limited mode of rendering destruction seems to have been of so little interest that the mediaeval artist preferred to rely on the spectator's knowledge to "decipher" the representation as one of decay or destruction. A rather characteristic example of an artist's shunning what to us would seem the crucial point, is the illustration in the *Bamberg Apocalypse* of the Fall of Babylon (*cecidit cecidit Babylon magna!*). At the right of the city we see the mourning fishermen, merchants and kings. From above the angel is coming down and a hand holding a thunderbolt appears from the clouds. The city of Babylon, shown in the usual way as an abbreviated conglomeration of buildings, enclosed in a wall, one gate standing wide open, is turned upside down, but otherwise quite intact. The open gate, we may assume, means "empty," "depopulated"; this is stressed by the people to the left, who have fled from the city. But no reason for "overturning" the city can be found in the ac-

---

[5] "To break: strictly, to divide; it signifies to humiliate as Prudentius in his Psychomachia 'God breaks all pride.' "—Ed.

tual text. The artist probably associated, by way of concordance, the passage from Isaiah: *"et erit Babylon, sicut subvertit dominus Sodomam et Gomorrham."*[6] With the help of this literary allusion a pictorial formula for destruction was found. Destruction was depicted as "integrity" with an inverted sign.

Integrity or perfection was the first of St. Thomas's categories of the beautiful. The second is the well-known classical postulate of symmetry, which St. Thomas defines as *debita proportio siue consonantia*. The third demand is that for *claritas: unde quae habent colorem nitidum, pulchra esse dicuntur*—"clarity, for on that account all things which have a lustrous (i.e. translucent) colour are regarded as beautiful." Clarity in the neo-Platonic philosophy of the Middle Ages signifies first of all the emanation of the divine nature, but there is no reason to doubt that this clarity could also be recognized in the visual configurations of translucent precious stones. . . .

Before illustrating in detail the insertion of antique gems in ecclesiastical objects, we may mention two forms of mediaeval preoccupation with precious stones, which have an indirect bearing upon our problem: the accumulation of gems in treasuries, and their magical use as amulets.

The economist who would want to give a strictly utilitarian reason for the mediaeval accumulation of treasures might find himself in grave difficulties. An extremely rare and well-shaped stone which travellers to distant regions had procured at great pains and expense might prove for all practical purposes about as "useful" as some exceptionally rare, exotic animal which had been transferred with very great care to Europe, where it was condemned to live artificially in a zoo. The comparison, far-fetched though it may sound, is actually borrowed from an historical account; for it is recorded that King Theodoric, after having his midday rest, used to visit "either his treasuries or his stables." The alternative sounds funny only as long as one assumes that his stables contained just a few horses or cows, but there can be no doubt that all sorts of rare and precious breeds were kept in them so that the pleasure and pride he felt in looking at these more or less fabulous specimens could be justly considered by him as equivalent to the enjoyment he derived from the jewels in his treasury. A sense of power and glory is conveyed to the possessor of these useless and—literally—far-fetched things; and the Church, as the chosen administrator of marvels in this world and the next, naturally vied with the secular potentates in the ambition to display her "Majesty" in a glamorous fashion. . . .

Of course it would be senseless to belittle the economic importance of these treasures. But shrewd economists have long recognized that at the root of many a standard of economic values lies a magical atavism, a superstition, which happens to be calculable in economic terms because in a given state of society it is in common to the majority of human beings. Of that nature is the love of precious stones, and to account for it by economic arguments alone is to put the cart before the horse. The accumulation of treasures, to be sure, is too amorphous a pleasure to reveal any direct affinity with aesthetic categories. But in dealing with the mediaeval aesthetics of precious stones one must not forget this magical root from which Beauty and Utility grew as separate stems, though they frequently intertwine.

[6] "And Babylon shall be as when the Lord overturned Sodom and Gomorrah."—Ed.

The use of amulets brings us one step nearer to our problem. For here it is not only the stone by itself but the sign engraved on it, which is supposed to have magical power. These signs are of purely pagan origin, but the mediaeval practitioners, who believed in their virtue, were able to blend their superstition with truly Christian sentiments. A characteristic text-book of this kind is preserved in the British Museum. Most of its prescriptions—they generally begin with *quando invenitur* [when it is found] —are meant to serve as medical charms, or else they promise to endow the owner of the amulet with super-human virtues and powers. . . .

The inheritance of power—a relatively simple process within the secular realm —was bound to become a more involved procedure within the domain of the Church. The Church admitted by implication the power of pagan charms and amulets; for before inserting ancient gems in ecclesiastical objects, she found it advisable to exorcise the evil forces residing in them. An example of a *benedictio* which is meant *expressis verbis* to be used for the exorcism of pagan gems is preserved in a thirteenth-century text. But though this is only a single instance, we may be certain that all the ancient stones which we find on Christian objects of cult, have undergone some form of sanctification. Perhaps it is not too daring to suppose that the emotion which expressed itself in this procedure, evolved from a state of fear to one of reverence—that reverence which St. Paul expressed in the words *"omnis creatura Dei bona est et nihil rejiciendum quod cum gratiarum actione percipitur; sanctificatur enim per verbum Dei et orationem."*[7]

So far from destroying the pagan charm the Church absorbed its power into her own, and sometimes even superimposed upon an ancient image a new type of magical function. . . .

In the actual process of adaptation we may distinguish two forms of reverence which at first glance seem to contradict each other:

(1) The careful preservation of the ancient relic in a setting which leaves it completely intact.

(2) The adjusting of the relic to the new setting by changing its form or its function, or both.

We shall see that both forms merge into each other by imperceptible degrees.

Of the first, the most impressive example is the famous "eagle vase" of Sugerius [d. 1151] abbot of St. Denis, which is now preserved in the Louvre. It is inscribed around the lip with a dedication of Sugerius to his church, and there can be no doubt that it was made under his supervision. The wings, claws, neck and head, of gilded silver, enshrine the antique (in this case probably Egyptian) core which is treated as a delicate treasure. We may take this as a typical instance of a purely "additive" procedure which clearly expresses the reverence for the antique unit by leaving it intact; *adaptavimus* [we have adapted] is the term used by Suger himself, while the creative act proper is described by him as a transposition ("transferre") of the *amphora* "*in aquilae formam*" [in the form of an eagle]. Needless to say the eagle, thus superimposed upon the antique relic, is meant as a symbol of Christ. . . .

Often a simple inscription or a mere association sufficed to transform a whole

---

[7] "For every creature of God is good, and nothing to be refused, if it be received with thanksgiving: for it is sanctified by the word of God and prayer."—Ed.

pagan scene into a biblical event. An antique intaglio of Athena and Poseidon, with a tree standing between them, was interpreted, according to the inscription, as a representation of Adam and Eve. The biblical words narrating the Fall of Man were added to the figures.

Leda with the swan—one of the favourite themes of the minor arts in Antiquity—appears on an ecclesiastical seal attached to a charter dated 1189. The inscription of the words (+SIGILL MAGIST ANDREE ARCHID SUESSION.) indicates that this was the personal seal of the archdeacon. Many other instances of the use of this image—among them one on the shrine of the Three Kings at Cologne—have been recorded. We know that the clerics, i.e. the *literati* of this time, were familiar with the classical story. So there can be no doubt that they understood the scene. It is not impossible that they placed upon it an *Interpretatio Christiana* [Christian interpretation]. In the "spiritual sense" of the exegetical writers, who admitted Danaë as a symbol of the immaculate conception, the union of Leda with the swan might well be interpreted as a scene foreshadowing the union of the Virgin with the Holy Ghost.

The desire to express in visible form the prophetic idea of "adumbration"—the foreshadowing of Christ in pre-Christian figures—may in some cases have been the motive which prompted the adaptation of ancient gems. In a gilded statuette of King David, which shows him holding a small figure of the Virgin, two ancient cameos have been inserted. The one—an antique sardonyx which, strangely enough, represented originally the head of Medusa—has been used for the head of David. The other, the figure of a lion, has been placed under the feet of the Virgin. King David, as the ancestor of Christ, foreshadows the coming

of the Saviour. He carries the figure of the Virgin because, as a member of the Old Covenant, he brings forth and supports the New. But the old order not only announces the new one, it also opposes it and is overcome by it. This vanquished part of the past is symbolized in the lion under the feet of the Virgin: *"Super aspidem et basiliscum ambulabis, et conculcabis leonem et draconem."*[8]

These words of the Psalm have often been quoted to illustrate the victory of Christianity over Paganism. The triumphant Church forces the pagan powers to submit to the new glory. Roman temples are transformed into Christian churches. Columns of pagan origin are made to support the roof under which the Christian god is worshipped. No doubt, the Christian adaptation of ancient cameos and intagli was also carried out in this spirit. Yet a very different lesson might be drawn from the statuette of King David and the Virgin Mary. An antique cameo was used not only for the vanquished lion, but also for the head of the King. The force which overcame and destroyed the old glamour was also the force which preserved it.

There is actual evidence that both forces could be combined in the activities of one person. The same Sugerius of Saint Denis who had taken such pains to preserve the intactness of the ancient stone of his "eagle vase," has left a record of a monumental project of "adaptation by destruction." In his *Liber de Consecratione* [Book of Consecration] which describes the various stages in the reconstruction of his church, he relates how, being in need of building material, he remembered the beautiful columns he had seen in Rome, particularly those

---

[8] "Thou shalt walk upon the asp and the basilisk: and thou shalt trample under foot the lion and the dragon." (Douay translation)—Ed.

in the "palace" of Diocletian. He says that it was only the wearisome procedure of shipping these pieces over the sea to France which eventually made him renounce his scheme of stripping them off. Had Sugerius carried out his plan, it would undoubtedly have been—in the mediaeval sense—a characteristic act of reverence. The modern romanticist may protest that by breaking up columns from the baths of Diocletian, Sugerius would have impaired recklessly the beauty of an antique site. Sugerius, however, considered the columns as units, beautiful in themselves, whereas the condition of the place as a whole, which the modern spectator enjoys as "atmosphere," ranged for him under the category of disintegration and therefore worthlessness.

It should be remembered that this point of view is quite familiar to the modern mind as far as paintings are concerned. Every restoration implies the destruction of those more recent strata of history which disfigure, so to speak, the original piece.

One of the few exceptions is the literary field, where the critic can happily restore an ancient text, without annihilating its "corrupted versions." It is fortunate, under these circumstances, that we should be able to interpret Sugerius' procedure in the light of a literary parallel. When Wibald of Stavelot had rebuilt the monastery of Corvey, he described in a letter to Manegold of Paderborn how he had placed on the pediment of the Southern porch, next to his own name, *"Grecis litteris illud de templo Apollinis: 'Scito te ipsum'."*[9] A Greek quotation transferred literally from the temple of Apollo to the monastery of Corvey is an exact analogy to the ancient columns which Sugerius proposed to transfer from the baths of Diocletian to the Church of St. Denis. The problem we have discussed in this article—the insertion of pagan relics into mediaeval settings—appears now as part of a much wider question: the form and function of quotations, both literary and pictorial, in the pattern of mediaeval life.

[9] "In Greek letters from the temple of Apollo: Know thyself."—Ed.

HANS LIEBESCHÜTZ (b. 1893) since 1957
has held the title of *Ausserplanmässiger* Professor
for medieval Latin literature at Hamburg
University, but he now lives in England and teaches
at Liverpool University. He has written both
on the cultural history of the Middle Ages
and on historiography in the nineteenth century.
His book on John of Salisbury, the most thorough
study yet published of humanism in the thought
of a medieval author, shows that John of Salisbury
quoted extensively from classical authors
without seeming to absorb the intellectual
context from which the quotations came.
Because John is usually considered the typical
example of Christian humanism in the twelfth
century, the study of the way he used classical authors
helps to explain the importance of classical
influence to the whole movement. Liebeschütz,
like Heckscher, finds classical concepts absent
from the twelfth century, filtered out by the
pervading influence of Christian thought, but
he does show that there was a precedent for this
selective use of classical sources in the writings
of the Church Fathers, especially those of
St. Jerome in the fifth century.*

▶ *A New Christian Humanism*

[That John of Salisbury's position in the history of humanism] is a complicated problem is evident at first sight. On the one hand, there is no doubt about the importance of John's Latin library as an influence in his life and writings. On the other hand, no reader of the *Policraticus* will fail to observe the gap which exists between the Englishman of the twelfth century and the writers and scholars who gave the word humanism its usual meaning during the Renaissance at the beginning of modern history. Moreover, we do not think that either John of Salisbury's championship of the Church or the limitations in his knowledge of ancient literature are sufficient to define his historical position. We must see how he modified and adapted, and finally understood, the clas-

* From Hans Liebeschütz, *Mediaeval Humanism in the Life and Writings of John of Salisbury.* (Studies of the Warburg Institute, Vol. 17), London, 1950, pp. 63–67, 82–85, 90–91. Footnotes omitted.

sical tradition. . . . We shall now [consider] the transformation which the educational and ethical ideas of antiquity underwent in John's work.

In his recommendation of what he calls philosophy, the product of Cicero's old age, John praises the Roman orator as the only great representative of "Latinitas nostra" [our Latinity] in the field of oratory equal, or even superior, to "Greek insolence," and remarks that Greek philosophers in contrast to "our" Seneca might be thought too ancient or their maxims not famous enough to be used as authorities. In another passage John distinguishes Terence by the same "our" from the Greek Menander and the Roman Plautus; he and his contemporaries knew the two latter authors only from hearsay or very scantily while they eagerly studied the former. The famous word of Bernard of Chartres,[1] cited and accepted by John in the *Metalogicon,* that the moderns, despite outstanding and even superior achievements, are dwarfs who stand on the shoulders of giants and may therefore be able to look a bit farther afield, illustrates John's attitude. The importance of antiquity for the author of the *Policraticus* is not based on the belief in the continuity of the Roman empire as we find it with the contemporary historians of the Hohenstaufen. John rather writes as a late pupil of great literary traditions of antiquity, and his feeling of membership of this community is founded on the common possession of learning and education. Reading alone brings about intimacy between antiquity and the contemporary. The Latin language is the only means of intercourse between Past and Present. Only the Latin book produces that type of educated man whom John thinks fit to master political tasks by moral and intellectual strength; Greek literature therefore, in spite of the overwhelming importance of its philosophers, seemed to belong to a strange and antagonistic world. What John knew and read of Plato and Aristotle was derived from Latin reports and Latin translations.

John of Salisbury's general conception of the continuity which existed between the ancient Latin world and his own period was practically the same as that which Bede[2] had already formulated as a direct expression of his people's great experiences in the century before his own. The establishment of the Roman Catholic Church meant a large influx of Roman ecclesiastical and cultural traditions into the northern country. Bede had derived from his patristic studies the conception of six world-ages, and he included Anglo-Saxon history in the last one. It was in consequence of this conception that Bede planned his great national work on the history of the English Church as a supplement to Eusebius' history of the ancient church, and also that he introduced to the West the system of dating from the era of the incarnation. His actual interest in the Roman and Byzantine emperors is essentially for purposes of chronology. The belief in the continuity or "renovation" of the Roman empire is obviously neither a necessary form of the allegiance of the Middle

---

[1] Bernard was master of the school of Chartres from 1114 to 1119 and chancellor of the school from 1119 to 1124. He is known only through the *Metalogicon* of John of Salisbury, who credits him with emphasizing the study of literature. —Ed.

[2] Bede (672–735) wrote the *Ecclesiastical History of the English People* and several treatises that gave an impetus to learning in England. —Ed.

Ages to Latin education and civilization, nor its oldest expression.

For a deeper understanding of John's views on Latin civilization we must go back beyond Bede to the decisive period of Latin patristics in the fourth century. In this period the synthesis between classical Latin literature and Christianity was achieved which remained the starting-point for Latin humanism in its whole development throughout the Middle Ages. Apart from Augustine,[3] St. Jerome was the most influential author represented in the libraries of the twelfth century. Among the Church Fathers, St. Jerome had been outstanding as a man of letters whose authority was not derived from any high ecclesiastical office but depended entirely on his learning and his literary abilities. He was the great representative of that kind of scholarship which the cultural conditions of the Latin Church required. Its doctrine and its form of worship, both based on Bible and tradition, had their origins in a foreign language. This circumstance gave the work of philologists, initiated in the Eastern Church by the great Origen,[4] a permanent place in the West. Literary studies which had formed the traditional basis of ancient rhetorical education were transferred from paganism to Christianity as an indispensable instrument for the learned interpretation of the Bible. The task induced a psychological atmosphere of a specific character based on the consciousness of individual knowledge and individual performance. St. Jerome, the letter-writer and controversialist, is the most definite and indeed the classic type of a man in a learned profession, because he is a man of lesser genius in the religious and practical spheres of life than are his great contemporaries. To him, as well as to Seneca's [*ca.* 4 B.C.–A.D. 65] letters to Lucilius, John of Salisbury refers when he dedicates his book on the courtiers' folly to the Chancellor Thomas.[5] John . . . makes ample use of Jerome's materials and expressions. It is perhaps possible to show that this actuality of St. Jerome for the clerk of Canterbury had its basis in a real affinity. St. Jerome professed Latin nationality in a sense which the English mediaeval scholar was able to accept. His allegiance to the world of "Latinitas" was no political one; the nation to which he belonged was the community of Christians. Hence he classed events in Roman history as foreign events whereas Biblical persons were for him his fellow-countrymen. And he shared the common ecclesiastical opinion of his period that this nation or community of Christians was composed of the most diverse elements without any regard to languages and traditions, as a result of the complete victory of the Church in the world. Nevertheless Jerome's special task was to serve the people of "our Latin Language." He wished to transmit to them the education of the Hebrews and the Greeks. And, especially in the struggle over the legacy of Origen in his later years, he was proud of the character of Latin

[3] The bishop of Hippo and Church Father who lived from 354 to 430, not the missionary to England of the same name who died about 607.—Ed.

[4] Origen (d. 254) was a Greek Church Father whose speculative writing was a source of the ideas that erupted in the Arian heresy of the early fourth century.—Ed.

[5] St. Thomas Becket (1118–1170) was a fellow student with John of Salisbury in the household of Archbishop Theobald of Canterbury. He was chancellor of King Henry II, a position he resigned when he became archbishop of Canterbury. John of Salisbury, although not present, was one who wrote of Becket's martyrdom.—Ed.

Christianity as a stronghold of orthodox belief. He looked upon himself as a guardian who had to take care that no Greek thought liable to endanger this purity of creed should be translated into Latin. Jerome's sympathy with Latinity was essentially the awareness of a connection with the literary tradition of a cultivated language. . . . When, 750 years later, John of Salisbury found the essence of Latin civilization in literature, and not in the remains of ancient Rome or in imperial titles, he was himself in complete agreement with St. Jerome's views and found his prophecies come true.

There is another point in which the great writer of the ancient Latin Church provided a precedent for his learned follower at Canterbury. St. Jerome's gloomy pronouncements on the fate of Rome and the empire, though certainly founded on the experiences of his age, were nevertheless not free from a certain bias. Jerome was a vigorous champion of ascetic life and ardently wished to win over to the ranks of virgins the daughters of the noble families with whom he had been well acquainted ever since his stay in Rome. Therefore he emphasized the ascetic life as the only refuge from the fatal dangers of the time. It is by contrast with this highly praised asceticism that Jerome draws his picture of worldly society, and he does not hide the fact that his attitude and his criticisms were meeting with opposition in the higher quarters of society. . . .

The society of Henry II's court is in no way identical with the society of the fourth century, and John of Salisbury is not the champion of a new asceticism; but the detachment of attitude is the same with both writers. Both are men of letters surveying from their writing-desks the activities of the world. John adopted from Jerome the habit of designating the typical representatives of court life by names taken from Latin literature. The man of the twelfth century draws near to the man of the fourth century in so far as he is intellectual enough to make society the subject of his contemplation.

St. Jerome was not only important for John of Salisbury as a critic of contemporary society, but he also became his model in the literary method of using parallel series of Biblical and classical illustrations to impress his views on his correspondents or on the readers of his polemical writings. From this point of view we can immediately gain an insight into John of Salisbury's method of dealing with ancient material. . . .

John came closest to ancient literature and philosophy when he set up the principle of moderation as the guiding rule of human life. In this his own character was in complete harmony with one important trend of ancient thought. Cicero's cautious scepticism in metaphysics and his Roman common sense in the discussion of ethical questions formed the real link between him and John.

We shall complete our survey of the significance of ancient philosophy for John by considering some of his quotations from Seneca whose importance as an authority in ethics he strongly emphasized. He is the foremost authority for John's argument that frugality is the key to the right life. In the passage to which John refers, Seneca deals with the enduring effects of his first experience of philosophical precepts in his youth. Under the influence of philosophy, for example, he had given up eating oysters and mushrooms, because he realized they were only stimulants enticing the satisfied to go on eating. From that time also he had given up the use of ointments, hot baths and wines. It is easy to see that this attitude on the part of man who, though living in the great world, had chosen to care for his own soul and that of others, was likely to rouse John's deep interest. He quotes Seneca s letters to Lucilius as a model of well-intentioned criticism upon which was based his own criticism of the Chancellor Thomas. John is not prepared to admit any criticism of Seneca except for reasons of style. He claims veneration for one who was recommended by his supposed correspondence with St. Paul and by a paragraph in St. Jerome's book on famous Christian writers in which the latter laid stress on the fact that Seneca was the tutor of Nero and suffered as a martyr for his moral firmness. We know that John had read this remark with interest, for the Plutarch whom he pictured in his *Institutio Trajani* was a copy of this great example. Seneca's theme is the individual who has to assert his dignity and his independence of fate, whatever its form and shape. . . . In a paragraph in which he probably points to this passage, John defines the boundaries between Christianity and philosophy. Some ancient philosophers had a certain knowledge of the immortality of the soul, but they had no adequate instruction about it; therefore they had to consider virtue as the ultimate object for which human beings ought to strive. Christianity does not make their belief invalid but is able to reconcile the various interpretations of virtue through the higher notion of God and the soul which it represents. From the Christian point of view the controversy between the different schools of philosophy lost its decisive importance, and the individual was left

free to choose between them without serious risk.

The pivot of John's Christian humanism was the question of moral education. . . .

John of Salisbury's use of ancient philosophy, so far as the moral and political problems of the *Policraticus* are concerned, is mainly restricted to the selection of such formulas from ancient writers as he considered gave concise expression to his own precepts for his contemporaries. "There is almost no pagan moralist whose work and sentences are more suitable for your use in all manner of affairs." Such is John's overall opinion of Seneca's importance. Here again we see that it is not John's intention to revive the systematic framework of ancient thought. On the contrary, we realize that his tendency in quoting from Seneca and especially from Cicero was to avoid all ideas which were concerned with the structural detail of classic thought. The casual use which John makes of quotations from Cicero's *De Re Publica* in his great political treatise is typical of his whole attitude towards ancient ethics.

As a preliminary to a discussion of John's conception of eloquence as an educational idea we shall first consider his master William of Conches' definition of this main discipline of the ancient schools. William of Conches had separated the art of eloquence with its three parts, grammar, rhetoric and dialectic, from theoretical and practical wisdom, and called it an appendix and instrument and not a species of philosophy. William defines eloquence as the ability to discourse on things known with well-turned phrases and sentences. He emphasizes the need for possessing both abilities, that of eloquence and that of philosophy, as weapons against the contemporary adversaries of liberal education. The marriage of Mercury and Philologia, the representative of wisdom, celebrated in the famous encyclopedia of Martianus Capella [d. 429], ought not to be dissolved. By this simile William intends to stress the necessity of a good philosophical education for men who are going to influence society by eloquence. John of Salisbury in his *Metalogicon* uses his master's definition and simile against groups of adversaries in the field of education, but he turns his thesis the other way round. He is afraid that the champions of dialectical disputation might bring about the downfall of all study of language except for the needs of logical terminology, and from this point of view he lays stress on the continuation of the alliance between Mercury and Philologia: whosoever attacks it, assaults in reality the foundations of society. The proper formalities, he says, which make contracts valid, as well as all orders issued between men, depend on the right use of words. No discipline of faith or morals is possible without the right understanding of speech which is the most important instrument. It is the connection of reason and word which has rallied and unified kingdoms and nations, and anyone who succeeded in severing this link would be a public enemy. It is in full accord with this point of view that the treatise, which John wrote to defend the propagation of studies among his contemporaries, deals in detail with grammar and dialectic as the two disciplines which give the right expression and the right order to human thought. But it seems a rather astonishing fact that the subject of the ancient curriculum most closely connected with eloquence,

namely rhetoric, is completely absent from John's discussion in the *Metalogicon*. However, the explanation is simple. The passage quoted above on the importance of a cultivated use of language does not refer to the pulpit but to the scriptorium. Ability in Latin grammar, style and logical training is, in John's mind, a necessary foundation for the man of letters. The drafting of documents and the writing of letters containing decisions on matters of administration and public life form the professional background to John of Salisbury's ideas on education. John belongs to the world of the Cathedral, where school and scriptorium, library and archives were the workaday habitat of learned churchmen who, in serving their bishop and chapter, are primarily concerned with administrative, political and spiritual activities. The feeling that business transactions took up time better applied to literary studies which John of Salisbury expresses so emphatically, may not have been rare among other masters in a similar situation. Nevertheless it was this combination of a wide range of activities which made the Cathedral and its clergy a dominant feature of twelfth-century life. . . .

Finally we shall attempt to define the relationship of John of Salisbury's humanism to some currents of thought and educational ideas prevalent in his own period. The main target of his polemic apart from the courtier class was the group of professional disputants and masters of the verbal technicalities of disputation for whom he showed his scorn by likening them to "Cornificus," the malicious critic of Virgil. It was against such people that he had written his *Metalogicon* as a defence of serious studies. "Cornificus" himself, the leader of the popular adversaries of literary education and serious learning, was described by John as a monster of ugliness both in appearance and character. But John does not hint at his real name nor does he give us any clear idea of his appearance, such as might enable us to recognize him and distinguish him from the others of his class whom he represents and who form the real object of attack in the *Metalogicon*. John traces the origin and spread of this group of professional disputants through the past two generations. He describes the opponents of literary culture in the England of 1159 as the pupils of that school of dialectic which despised the reading of ancient poets and historians. Such men had only to learn the dialectical terms of their masters' invention and their own in order to become forthwith masters themselves. In this way they had, about 1145, temporarily secured predominance in Chartres and Paris in spite of the resistance of the most prominent professors of their time. There is a similar description of this unfair competition in the prologues of William of Conches' *Philosophia* and in his *Dragmaticon* of 1147. Their eventual defeat showed them to be malicious slanderers whose bitter tongues were directed against any contemporary scholar of importance. In his *Metalogicon* John explains the fact that this type of man was to be met in every walk of life as resulting from their dispersion following their defeat in the academic world. Some, as monks, were converted to the regular life; among their number were some who sincerely renounced the vanities of their youth while others turned out hypocrites. Another group of these disappointed students of dialectics went to Salerno and Montpellier to become doctors of medicine with the same rapidity as that with which formerly they had become philosophers. There they paraded their knowledge by quoting Hippocrates and Galen, of whom nobody had ever heard, in order to create confidence in their prescriptions. But in reality they were only interested in hard cash. In consequence of their ignorance of philosophy they were, John maintains, quite unable to penetrate the secrets of nature, and through their lack of education in languages they would never be able to understand medical literature. Other people of this type which John personifies in Cornificus became business men and thought only of making money. They lent money at interest and were afraid of nothing but poverty. Finally, another way of escape was to secure a livelihood as a courtier in a great lord's household. John has to admit that he also belongs to this profession, but he points in self-defence to his discussion of the courtier's way of life in the *Policraticus*.

This critical discussion of the influence of the professional disputant and dialectician on contemporary life expresses John's view that the purpose of academic study is to make a man really fit for his activities in Church and State, and one of his charges against dialectic training is that it tends to find its object in itself. On the other hand, the purely technical routine of book-keeping on a small or large scale which was the function of the contemporary clerk in current administration, was to John's mind devoid of all those human values which are imparted by a liberal education. This is the basis for the parallel which John draws between the empty art of professional dialectic which can be practised without any concrete knowledge, and the routine activities of the household officers. John who had secured employment in administration as a philosopher and man of letters, defended his own career emphatically against the more modern method of training through the business-routine in the office which, however, was destined to prevail. The great business man who about two decades after the appearance of John's *Policraticus* wrote the famous treatise on the exchequer, the first spokesman of the new class of officials, maintained that administrative practice was at least as valuable a training-ground as the study of Plato's abstract doctrine. He was thus John's exact counterpart, representing a tendency the importance of which John had perceived very keenly. John resisted this new tendency; whereas the author of the dialogues stood as a champion of what in fact proved to be an important vehicle of social progress.

ÉTIENNE GILSON (b. 1884) has written many
books and articles on the history of medieval
philosophy, of which *The Spirit of Medieval
Philosophy* (1932) is probably the most widely
known. For many years before his retirement
he was director of studies at the Pontifical
Institute at Toronto; he also taught at the
universities of Lille, Strasbourg, and Paris. Gilson's
major contribution to an interpretation of the twelfth
century is his book *Héloïse and Abélard* (1938),
which grew out of his attempt to deal with the
question of humanism in the twelfth century.
Prior to this book his views on medieval and
Renaissance humanism had appeared in the influential
article used for the following selections. In it
he developed his thesis that medieval humanism
reached its height in the philosophical works
of St. Thomas Aquinas in the thirteenth century.*

Philosophical Humanism in the Twelfth Century

Our teaching of history follows a convenient system of classification which places events into carefully separated epochs: antiquity, the Middle Ages, the Renaissance, modern times. It would be somewhat absurd to maintain that in reality nothing corresponds to these divisions, and I do not mean to take this view. But it is rather naïve to neglect to take into account—as it seems to me certain scholars do—that the continuity of history is not readily fragmented into segments as distinct as our concepts. This is why it is perhaps not bad from time to time to put the accepted classifications to the test of actual events, to submit our own concepts to a test of resistance to

see up to what point they are capable of supporting the weight of reality without giving way. This becomes more necessary as the number of known facts increases from day to day, both in history and in science, and in history as in science the right of theories to existence is in direct proportion to their ability to interpret events. It is to a critique of this kind that I wish to submit the traditional idea of the Renaissance. . . .

The development of science is generally considered to be one of the essential features of the Renaissance, and rightly so. The sixteenth century accomplished more in this development than all the preceding fifteen centuries to-

* Étienne Gilson, "Humanisme médiéval et renaissance," *Les Idées et les lettres* (Paris, 1932), pp. 171–172, 174–176, 188–193. Translated by Christine Hyatt. Footnotes omitted.

gether. I do not believe that these fifteen centuries achieved nothing or that the sixteenth century achieved everything it is credited with. Nevertheless, its contribution remains enormous, preponderant, and it will never be denied it; there was then a beginning, or a new beginning, which Robert Grosseteste, Roger Bacon, William of Moerbeke, Witelo,[1] and others were able to foresee and prepare for, but which none of them knew how to direct in the right way. It is quite a different matter, I believe, with that other essential element of the Middle Ages, known as humanism, for if there was no medieval science in the strict sense of the word, there was certainly a medieval humanism, in relation to which the humanism of the Renaissance was, in certain respects, only the continuation and the expansion.

The traditional views of history are far from agreeing with this conclusion. Quite the contrary, not content with affirming that the Middle Ages took no interest in ancient learning, the historians sometimes go so far as to demonstrate that they could not have done so and that humanism would have been a complete negation of all they stood for. Humanism, being both the veneration of Greek and Roman antiquity and the love of the strength and beauty of form for its own sake, is in short the corresponding love of the strength and the dignity of nature and of man as such. *Contemptus saeculi* [Contempt for the world], it is said, is the Middle Ages; the value of nature and of man, that is

the Renaissance. Complete antithesis. Since then, according to M. Roger in a book now a classic, "How could it have been possible, in principle, to attach a value to knowledge or to talents which after all perceived only man, only the city of Rome, only the good things and the joys of this world, in a society in which one's whole life, both public and private, hung on a single interest, that of God, on whom the destiny of the world and the fate of each individual human being are dependent for eternity? . . ." One could not find a better piece of evidence to prove that the people of the Middle Ages did not have the right to love learning, but supposing they did, what are we to do? Alcuin tells us.[2]

To be born in such happy times when generosity of heart and justness of spirit are sufficient to perform great things; to see what must be done, to do it, and to die leaving behind rich works for posterity—there is no destiny more worthy of envy. This was the destiny of Alcuin. Of the millions of Europeans who live and die without giving him a thought, there is not one in whom his thought does not live on, but of the rare visitors who frequent the solitude where this reserved spirit watches, few leave without dedicating to him a grateful affection. . . .

[Gilson continues to develop the thesis that Alcuin transmitted Greco-Roman culture to posterity by his dream of pressing science and literature into the service of the Church. This approach was made a reality by writers in the twelfth century who took up the theme of the translation of studies from Athens and Rome to France of their own day, exemplified by writings of Bernard of Chartres, Chrétien de Troyes, Bernard

---

[1] Robert Grosseteste (d. 1253) and Roger Bacon (d. 1292) contributed to physics, especially in optics, and to scientific methodology. William of Moerbeke (1215–1286) made Aristotle's works available to the West in his Latin translation. Witelo (b. *ca.* 1220–1230) was a Polish scientist influenced by the Neoplatonic theories of light. His work also provides an example of a growing interest in astronomy.—Ed.

[2] Alcuin (735–804) was a leader in the revival of learning under Charlemagne.—Ed.

Silvestris, and Hildebert of Lavardin.]

Two objections can be made to texts of this sort: first, that they were the accomplishment of isolated individuals, and, second, that the classic century of the Middle Ages, the thirteenth, did not produce anything of a similar kind. Neither objection, let us acknowledge, appears conclusive.

First, it is not true that our humanists were isolated. From Alcuin to Hildebert the line was a continuous one, and each of them was someone's pupil and someone's master. But the best evidence that the movement was widespread is found in the implacable opposition it encountered, in the twelfth century as in the seventeenth, and as in the twentieth. The Middle Ages had already had their dispute between the ancients and the moderns, and this could not have occurred had there been no truly deep and widespread love of antiquity. The moderns of the twelfth century are the Cornificians, whom John of Salisbury ridiculed so humorously, and like all moderns they were utilitarians. Their demands were for logic and law, because these led to lucrative professions—today they would be asking for applied mathematics and chemistry—but they cared not at all for Horace and Cicero for they served no practical use. Long live the youths who know all the answers from birth and need no one to guide them! The humanists are fools. . . .

Medieval humanism was indeed a profound and extensive movement and, it may be added, far from disappearing in the thirteenth century, it became more intensified, at the same time taking on quite a different form. From being literary it became philosophical. The importance of this fact and the lack of rec-

ognition given to it are such that they are worth stressing.

The specialization of our studies and of our teaching is perhaps a necessary evil, but it is a real evil and its ill effects can never be sufficiently denounced. Every teacher tailors to his own use a portion of reality, and he then naturally believes that reality is made up of pieces and fragments. It is the "literary men" who wrote the history of humanism; how could they ever imagine it as being anything other than literary? What we do not know does not exist—this is the method. Nevertheless, one would have to be extremely naïve to imagine that the love of antiquity is identical with the love of ancient literature, for antiquity was something other, and far more, than a literary tradition. Humanism is cruelly mutilated when it is reduced to the cult of form for form's sake, which it never was, and when it is deprived of the cult of ideas, from which it has never been separated.

But as soon as classical philosophy is reintegrated into Humanism the whole problem takes on another aspect. The Middle Ages in general, and the thirteenth century in particular, are criticized for their obsession with Aristotle; admitting—*dato non concesso* [for the sake of argument]—that there is some truth in this, the Middle Ages cannot, however, be criticized at the same time for two completely contradictory failings: failure to have appreciated the value of antiquity and obsession with Aristotle. If there is a typical Greek, it must be this disciple of Plato, this philosopher of form and space, this intellectual who makes God into pure thought and thought of his own thought. If then one admits that, over and above the humanism of letter and form there is a humanism of the spirit, with all that this implies of trust in the stability, the value, and the efficacy of nature and of man, one can no longer fail to recognize that in assimilating Aristotle the Middle Ages assimilated Hellenism itself, with what is eternally valid in it, and in so doing effected a revolution far more profound than that of the art of writing: a revolution in the art of thinking.

This was the work of St. Thomas Aquinas. To take him for a humanist is to misunderstand him and to diminish him strangely; he is something quite different and much more than this, but that the immense edifice of Thomism contains humanism as one of its appurtenances is in my view evidence itself. To compare, to expound, and to spread abroad across Europe the ethics and the teachings of Aristotle did much more for the propagation of ancient thought than could be done by the imitation, even a successful one, of a few verses of Homer or Sophocles. No one has ever wondered what influence St. Thomas Aquinas might have had on the Italian Renaissance; yet there could be something worth investigating, and probably discovering, here. Thomism not only brought about a restoration of the idea of nature, the idea that the Reformation was to deny against the assertion of the Middle Ages, but also a justification of man and of life in what they have that is rightly human. St. Thomas does not glorify work for its own sake; he glorifies it only for the sake of the worker, but he glorifies it all the same and for the very reason that it bears witness. He would not have been surprised by the intense vitality of the Italian Renaissance, or by the magnificence of the princely courts, or by the development of art; he predicted them, foresaw them, made ready for their coming. The theory of magnificence precedes Lorenzo

the Magnificent,[3] and it is to be found in the *Summa theologica*. It is St. Thomas who extols magnanimity in his reasoned treatise on true honor; he extols it so greatly that he goes so far as to make a sin of its opposite, meanness of soul, and let us see whether his preamble disregards the value of nature: *omne illud quod contrariatur naturali inclinationi est peccatum, quia contrariatur legi naturae.*[4] The sin of the coward is that he does not succeed in achieving full self-realization, in completely realizing his potentialities: *pusillanimus deficit a propositione suae potentiae.*[5] Why then be astounded that he also extols the Magnificent, that is, the Prince who, living and acting in princely fashion, knows how to do what a prince has to do: to construct and to expend? For magnificence is strength; it dominates the opposite vices, which hold the sovereign back from acting according to his essence; it prevents him from foundering in an excess of absurd extravagance or of sordid avarice; it turns him into a true sovereign.

Can one believe that the Italian Renaissance had not heard this glorification of the virtue of strength, with the magnanimity and the magnificence which derive from it? The only new thing it could do was to separate them from their supernatural purpose by attributing them to man alone instead of subordinating them to God. It managed to overthrow their order and to pervert it, but it could not invent them, for they were already there, beneath its eyes,

[3] Lorenzo de' Medici (1449–1442), a ruler of Florence at the height of the Renaissance, was famous for his patronage of the arts.—Ed.

[4] "Everything that is contrary to natural inclination is sin because it is contrary to the law of nature."—Ed.

[5] "The fainthearted man by definition fails to reach his potentiality."—Ed.

classified, defined, and incorporated in Catholic dogma by Thomist philosophy. The difference between the Renaissance and the Middle Ages is not a difference by excess but by default. The Renaissance, such as it is depicted, is not the Middle Ages plus man, but the Middle Ages less God, and the tragedy is that in losing God the Renaissance would lose man himself, but this would be another and a long account to relate.

If, then, one considers humanism in the fullness of its essence, and in its spirit no less than in its letter, far from saying that it suffered a setback in the thirteenth century one should say that this century saw its full establishment. But one would be mistaken in thinking that literary humanism disappeared during this period. Although its history is still little known, one can predict with some certainty that those who will look for the course of its development in thirteenth-century Italy will not fail to find it there.

One of the early books about the intellectual changes of the twelfth century was G. Robert, *Les Écoles et l'enseignement de la théologie pendant la première moitié du XIIe siècle* published in 1909. When a new edition was planned, it was found that progress in medieval studies had been so rapid that a simple revision would not suffice. Therefore three members of L'Institut d'Études Médiévales d'Ottawa— GÉRARD PARÉ (b. 1906), ADRIEN BRUNET (b. 1906), and PIERRE TREMBLAY (b. 1909)— undertook to rework completely the older study and to incorporate advances in knowledge about "the Christian humanism of the medieval renaissance." Their book, *The Renaissance of the Twelfth Century: Schools and Teaching,* published in 1933, is virtually a new work inspired by the pioneering effort of Robert. Their sympathy for the period and for the teachings of St. Thomas Aquinas is evident in their approach to the question of the relation between the twelfth-century renaissance and scholasticism.*

Scholasticism as a Renaissance

It is no longer a paradox to speak of "renaissance" with regard to the century which saw the birth of scholasticism; it has even become the stereotype according to which encyclopedias and textbooks now classify the literary and doctrinal history of the twelfth century. The account . . . of the academic organization, its new conditions, and methods of instruction testifies in its own way to a sudden increase of intellectual labor and a refining of education, which were promoted more and more by the emancipa-

tion of the rural classes, the establishment of towns, the extension of commercial exchanges, geographical discoveries, and the movement of travelers. We come now to the very soul of this movement: conditioned by this social, political, and academic economy, the intellectual life tried in its turn to spiritualize it by putting it to its own service. The University of Paris, in 1200, was to be the natural fruit of this vigorous force, securing a little for its own benefit the life parceled out among the cultural centers

---

* From Gérard Paré, Adrien Brunet, and Pierre Tremblay, *La Renaissance du XIIe siècle: les écoles et l'enseignement* (Paris and Ottawa: L'Institut d'Études Médiévales, 1933), pp. 138–140, 142–143, 188–189, 206–208. Translated by Christine Hyatt. Footnotes omitted.

of the twelfth century, until, before the middle of the thirteenth century, it was inspiring and inciting the founding of corporate university bodies on similar lines throughout Europe.

Before we distinguish and analyze in themselves the diverse tendencies and schools of thought which made up this intellectual life and held it together in the first half of the twelfth century, it is important to outline its general aspect and, determining the meaning of this intellectual movement, to place this "medieval Renaissance" in the general history of Latin civilization in Europe. The orientation of its first aspirations and its first measures was to determine its evolution, and the factors that then intervened were to involve by their more or less unstable balance, by their conflict or their agreement, its subsequent fate: grammar and logic, humanities and dialectics, the pre-eminence of *trivium* (letters) over *quadrivium* (the sciences), the discovery of Aristotle and the disappearance of Plato—all these elements, acting and reacting, were to end by leading the humanist "renaissance" of the twelfth century to the scholasticism of the thirteenth. Still Renaissance—this must be emphasized—for it is the same cult of antiquity and the same impassioned ardor; it is, and still more so, the same candid faith in reason, right into the sphere of religion; but between humanism (grammar, letters) and the natural sciences (*quadrivium*), up to that time in harmony, triumphant logic was to inject in one-sided fashion this intellectual ardor, endowing philosophy and theology with an admirable instrument but, for at least a century, almost drying up the taste for fine style and eloquence and eliciting the antimedieval reaction of the Renaissance. An eddy which gave the appearance of a breach in

the times for a completely new beginning after ten centuries of darkness. But history, in reviewing the course of events, regained the continuity of reality and left off bending classifications and convenient concepts according to the complex reality of events.

If in fact one speaks of a medieval Renaissance in the twelfth and thirteenth centuries, between the Carolingian Renaissance and the Renaissance of the fifteenth century, it is not in the manner of a spurt of culture between two univocal eruptions, or as an attempt at ancient culture, abortive like the first before the third should be successful; it is, according to quite individual traits, like a very original stage in the course of a continuous cycle, which from beginning to end is a reconquest of the capital of ancient civilization. And this progressive conquest, which took place on Christian ground, found itself for that very reason profoundly transforming the object of its discovery, and it is a fact that this constant effort caused a continuous thread to run through the whole intellectual life of the Middle Ages, albeit with many impediments. "Three great waves in the continuous flow of classical influences during the Middle Ages."...[1]

It is between these two summits that the Renaissance of the twelfth and thirteenth centuries is placed, of which the particular objects were to be—in succession and in different spheres—Roman law and Greek philosophy. One must most certainly not yield on any account to the contempt, conscious or unconscious, with which the literary production of the twelfth and thirteenth centuries, particularly the Latin literature, has long been regarded; we must recall,

[1] Quoted from Louis J. Paetow, *A Guide to the Study of Medieval History.*—Ed.

summarily at least, both its power and its quality. Here as elsewhere the isolation in which "men of letters," "philosophers," and let us add, "men of science" (for Greek and Arabic science was then in the same category as philosophy) worked, each on his own, resulted in the disintegration of a cultural complex into elements from then on in a state of decay and disharmony. But finally, the intellectual intoxications of renewal, in their universal rationalism, took their nourishment, from among the ancient sources, more from Roman law and Greek philosophy than from Ovid or Cicero: the discovery of *Pandects*; the cultivation of the *Digest*; the intensive work of Irnerius and his successors at Bologna; the benefit reaped from it by the canonist Ivo of Chartres.[2] There were so many sensational elements in the twelfth century, as much from the scientific point of view as from the cultural point of view and the ecclesiastical-theological point of view; then, a worthy parallel, a century later, there was the no less sensational entry of Aristotle, in various successive "waves," the last of which, at the height of the thirteenth century, in Paris, consummated the definitive establishment of Greek thought in western understanding and in Christian theology. Two areas then, of very different aims and adherents, but pervaded by the same enthusiasm, in the same spirit, with the same impregnation of Roman order and Greek illumination: both equally

expanding and stimulating the academic life, the law by the careers it made open, Greek philosophy by the internal conflicts it stirred up.

Whatever one's opinion of the ideological content of these weighty contributions and these impassioned exploitations, one cannot deny that there is here clearly a decisive stage of "Renaissance" of antiquity; and if one wishes to weigh a similar object of culture by the weight of ideas and not by the weight of rhetoric, it is equally undeniable that the Renaissance of the twelfth-thirteenth centuries penetrates to the depths of man before the Renaissance of the fifteenth century, all other things being equal. . . .

Perhaps one might be tempted (it is even accepted as obvious in certain conceptions of intellectual life in the Middle Ages) to class equally among the antihumanists those who, taking their inspiration from St. Augustine's *De doctrina christiana*, conceived the whole program of instruction in the seven arts as a preparatory study to theology. Actually, this was to be, in the thirteenth century and for a long time, the order according to which the medieval university was to be constructed, an organization of universal learning, presided over by theology. But apart from considering as the very definition of humanism a culture cut off from every religious ideal, there remains only an extremely flexible draft, and this was the meaning of the measure and of the progress of medieval humanism, instituted by the Renaissance of the twelfth century, to constitute inside this complete synthesis of human knowledge, and without diminishing the human need and the magnitude, a hierarchy and an autonomy of diverse disciplines.

It was in the twelfth century that this

---

[2] *Pandects* is another name for the *Digest*. The *Digest*, containing the legal opinions of Rome's most important jurists, discussed the principles of Roman law and was, for this reason, the most useful part of Justinian's *Corpus Juris Civilis* for the revived study of Roman law in the eleventh and twelfth centuries. Irnerius (d. 1130) led this revival at the university of Bologna. Ivo of Chartres (*ca.* 1040–1116) applied methods developed for the study of Roman law to the study of the law of the Church.—Ed.

doctrine of the hierarchy of the sciences, the true wisdom, *sapientia*, was formed, not only in the thought of the masters but in the reality of the institutions. The Carolingian "Renaissance" had primed it, in spirit and in deed; the humanism, the philosophy, and the theology of the twelfth century, then of the thirteenth, perfected its elaboration. Honorius of Autun, in his *De animae exsilio et patria*,[3] depicts man as an exile: his exile is ignorance, his country is wisdom; to reach it, he must follow a road that runs through ten cities; the seven liberal arts, physics, mechanics, and economics are the cities. "If believers are allowed to read works that discuss the liberal arts and the books of the ancients," wrote Abelard, "it is so that, being acquainted thanks to them with grammar, rhetoric, and logic as well as the natural sciences, we might be capable of understanding everything pertaining to the meaning and the beauty of the Scriptures, and that we might be able to uphold it or attain to the truth of it." John of Salisbury declares in his *Entheticus* that the science of the Scriptures is the queen of the sciences and that all the others must attribute their concurrence to her. Abelard and John of Salisbury, each in their order, were among those humanists whose culture we have valued.

This academic notion finds its doctrinal expression within the system of theology: philosophical speculation, "dialectics," are taken up in it as means for elaborating the faith into a rational discipline: philosophy is here—not in itself in its proper subject, but in relation to this faith in work—*ancilla theologiae* [handmaiden of theology]. A celebrated formula and one so badly understood, on the one hand by certain historians of philosophy who see in it an exploitation of philosophy, and on the other by many theologians who, perverted by the scholastic "baroque" of pseudo-humanism, have lost the feeling of this friendly trust of faith in the reason to which it gives life: *fides quaerens intellectum. . . .*[4]

We have left a "Renaissance"; here we are in the midst of "scholasticism." This would be an untenable paradox according to the common usage of the words if our analyses, our proceedings, step by step, had not led us to verify, in its expansions and its retractions, its successive and never complete triumphs, the great movement of cultural and spiritual renewal, created and sustained, throughout the whole of the Middle Ages in the West, by the conquest of the capital of the ancients. Categories and stereotypes can be done away with as long as the coherence and the continuity of history and thus its intelligibility are made clear even in its most profound evolutions.

What then is the meaning of the word scholastic, an epithet so often coupled with such a philosophy, such a theology, such an art, such a method, such a mental structure? and this by an implicit reference to the "Middle Ages" in counterbalance to the Renaissance.

This is not the place to review the case of this equivocal word. But at least one or other of the features which is bound, in every hypothesis, to enter into the construction of the concept of scholasticism, will emerge from our investigation of schools and instruction in the twelfth century.

Scholasticism is born at the heart of a Renaissance. The first testimony of this,

---

[3] Honorius of Autun wrote *Concerning the Exile and Fatherland of the Mind* in the early twelfth century.—Ed.

[4] "Faith seeking understanding" was a cardinal principle of St. Anselm's (1033–1109) philosophy. —Ed.

the most unassuming but the least contestable, is that the academic and cultural teaching was based on *lectio*, the reading of texts, texts recognized by authority in the schools, glossed, annotated, disputed, interpreted in every sense, but recognized as works of a wonderful past which had to be brought to life again as norms of intellectual, literary, and scientific life. *O Roma nobilis!* [O noble Rome!] Benefice or servitude, it matters little; the psychology of the "artists," the masters of the first half of the twelfth century, is made up of curiosity, enthusiasm, ingenuousness, experienced by minds on discovering more or less suddenly a new world. This world, as we have said, had in reality been revealed for a long time, and the "renaissance" was not an unheralded event devoid of any context; but, around the year 1100, there was a bursting forth in an afflux of new texts and of ideas then unheard of. The process of the *lectio* [reading of texts], thus applied to the *auctores* [authors] of antiquity, is the academic index of renewal; and because this renewal was founded on ancient culture, in minds in ferment with communal life, the awakening occurred according to this estimation of human values, this trust in reason, this veneration of form, which make up a humanism.

More profoundly than with a scholarly system, it is in truth with an intellectual work based on imitation that we have to deal, imitation in the broadest sense of the word: not only adoption of methods of literary composition, the acceptance of rules and the admiration of models, but recourse to the sources of beauty, of truth, of science, of scholarship, which nourish the fervor of minds and the curiosity of intellects. Indeed, personalities remain the creators of their destiny and their works: Chrétien de Troyes imitates Ovid, but he is the writer of romances of courtly love; St. Thomas espouses Aristotle but the Thomist philosophy is rooted in other metaphysical intuitions. But at last an acquired stock enters into composition and cultivation; it is not pure creation and is sometimes knowledge acquired from books. Scholasticism proceeds from a renaissance; it yields the fruits of it and bears the weaknesses.

If we carry on the analysis of this mental structure, various cases of which are shown in the history of human societies, elements will intervene which, individualizing this renaissance, will make up the face of this budding scholasticism. In its humanism the taste and refinement of truth inspires and guides aesthetic preoccupations, and this would only bring humanism to its normal perfection if in fact in the circumstances and the contingencies mentioned, this taste had not been embodied, cramped, and restricted in logic. As a method of discussion this logic, by generalizing in "real" attainments, corrupts authentic intellectualism; expediently making uniform the activities of the mind, it causes the acute sense of the difference and the specificity of the methods to be lost, which the first generations of the renaissance perceived from the first and which Albert the Great and St. Thomas were to proclaim so vigorously in the thirteenth century.

In his four volumes entitled *The Monastic Order
in England* (1940) and *The Religious Orders
in England* (1950–59) DOM DAVID KNOWLES
(b. 1896) produced a definitive history of
the religious life in England from the tenth to
the seventeenth century. His dedication to
scholarship had been encouraged when he
entered Downside Abbey as a Benedictine monk.
In 1947 he became Professor of Medieval History
at Cambridge University, and is now Emeritus
Regius Professor of Modern History. The felicitous
style and breadth of learning that distinguish
his works are evident in his article on humanism
in the twelfth century. As opposed to the
previous two selections, Knowles concludes that
the humanism of the twelfth century declined
in the face of the scholasticism of the thirteenth.*

The Difference Between
Scholasticism and Humanism

The two centuries that follow the millennium, which have been so closely
studied by the historians of politics, economics and art, have perhaps not yet
yielded up all their secrets in the realm
of cultural life. It is only too easy to regard the medieval period as a prelude
and preparation for the modern world,
and to consider the history of Western
civilization as that of an ordered progress
towards the material and intellectual
perfection of man; within the medieval
centuries themselves it is equally invit-
ing to discover a steady and straightfor-
ward evolution from barbarism to enlightenment. Yet even in constitutional,
legal and economic history where such a

view is least misleading, the conception
of an ordered and unhalting progress,
familiar to Victorian writers, must re-
ceive modification in more than one respect; in the history of intellectual development and the changes of religious
sentiment any idea of an unfaltering advance is wholly false.

This, perhaps, is particularly true in
respect of the first great flowering of culture in Western Europe which began
shortly after the year 1000. This age,
save for its artistic life, had until recently
been unduly neglected by historians of
thought. The great moral and intellectual leaders—Anselm, Abelard and Bernard, and their lesser contemporaries

* From Dom David Knowles, "The Humanism of the Twelfth Century," *Studies*: An Irish
Quarterly Review (Talbot Press, Dublin 1, Ireland), XXX (1941), pp. 43–45, 46–48, 55–58.

such as Peter the Venerable[1] or John of Salisbury—were indeed familiar figures, but they had been treated only in isolation; and even during the last twenty years, when the various schools of medieval philosophy and theology have at last attracted something of the attention they deserve, there has been a tendency to regard the eleventh and twelfth centuries as but a dawning, a prelude, to the thirteenth, the "greatest of centuries," which opened with Innocent III and St. Francis, which saw the earliest and purest masterpieces of Gothic architecture spring into being at Chartres, at Paris, at Salisbury and at Westminster, which embraced all the glories of scholastic theology, and which closed upon the year in which Dante, waking in the hillside forest, passed in imagination through the realms beyond the grave. In consequence, even those who, like the late Professor Haskins, have done most to extend our knowledge of the twelfth century or who, like Denifle and Ehrle and Mandonnet and Grabmann, have studied the growth of the universities, the origins of scholasticism and the prehistory of the friars—even these, when treating of earlier years, have given their attention to the seeds that were still to bear fruit rather than to the ripe ears of the summer's harvest. Yet to a careful observer the latter half of the twelfth century appears as a decline as well as a dawn, and as he looks back over the brilliant creative achievement of the hundred years between 1050 and 1150 and

[1] St. Anselm of Bec and Canterbury (1033–1109) used dialectical argument to support theological positions known by faith. An example is his ontological proof for the existence of God. The Bernard who is meant is St. Bernard of Clairvaux (1091–1153). Peter the Venerable (*ca.* 1122–1156) was the abbot of Cluny. He attempted to mediate between Abelard and St. Bernard, and provided a refuge for Abelard in his last days.—Ed.

notes its deep and sympathetic humanism, which anticipated to an extraordinary degree much that is considered typical of the age of the Medici and of Erasmus, he becomes sensible of a very real change and declension between 1150 and 1200 which helped to make the culture of the thirteenth century, for all its intense speculative force and abiding power, less universal, less appealing and, in a word, less humane than what had gone before.

It is the purpose of these pages to direct attention to the earlier years, to the brilliant and original creative energies of the late eleventh century, and to the wide and sympathetic humanism which between 1050 and 1150 made its appearance for the first time in Western Europe. This first great rebirth—the proto-Renaissance as it has sometimes been called by historians of art and architecture—took place earlier than is generally supposed; the movement reached maturity between 1070 and 1130; it changed and declined in the fifty years between the death of St. Bernard and the pontificate of Innocent III, and the intellectual atmosphere of the thirteenth century which followed, though it was in some ways more rare, more bracing and more subtle, lacked much of the kindly warmth and fragrant geniality of the past. The culture of the schools was, in fact—to drop the language of metaphor—without many of the elements that make a society fully humane, and that the preceding age had possessed for a time and subsequently lost.

The three notes of the new humanism, which set the great men of the eleventh and twelfth centuries apart from those who had gone before and those who came after, may be put out as: first, a wide literary culture; next, a great and what in the realm of religious sentiment would be called a personal devotion to certain figures of the ancient world; and, finally, a high value set upon the individual, personal emotions, and upon the sharing of experiences and opinions within a small circle of friends.

Since the ideas and emotions thus shared were often of a religious or, at least, of a philosophical character, and since the writers were in every case men who wrote little or nothing that could be called pure poetry or secular literature, the fundamental humanism of their outlook has been overlooked or, at best, has been recognized only in those who, like John of Salisbury or Hildebert of Chartres, were classical scholars of an eminence that would attract notice in any age. In one celebrated case, indeed, it has been obscured by the persistent attempts that have been made to romanticize the past in a totally unhistorical fashion. Nevertheless, the men of the early twelfth century, if they are regarded with attention and sympathy, show themselves as possessed of a rare delicacy of perception and warmth of feeling. It is to the sixteenth century, not to the thirteenth, that one looks for the spiritual kin of Anselm, of John of Salisbury, and of Héloïse.[2]

The hall-mark of the revival, and the accomplishment that was most widely possessed by all whom it affected, was a capability of self-expression based on a sound training in grammar and a long and often loving study of the foremost Latin writers. The great ecclesiastics, one and all, who flourished between 1030 and 1180, could express themselves not only in fluent, correct and often elaborate language, but also in phrases and sentences of true dignity and eloquence. Peter Damian, John of Fécamp, Anselm, Abelard, Bernard, William of Malmesbury, Peter the Venerable, John of Salisbury—all these,[3] and a hundred others, were masters of a flexible style and a wide vocabulary; they can be read with ease and pleasure; they are capable of giving adequate expression to their ideas and emotions, and do not fail to do so. Indeed, a student of the period comes to take this for granted—just as, in the use of contemporary manuscripts, he takes for granted the uniform, clear and beautiful script. Yet all this is in contrast alike to the age which had gone and to that which was to follow. Even the most learned men of the previous century, such as Abbo of Fleury, are narrow in the range of their ideas and awkward in their utterance; in England, among those who write Latin, the ideas are still less mature and the expression often laboured to the point of incomprehensibility. As for the century that came after, it may seem paradoxical to suggest that the great churchmen and thinkers of the age were inarticulate; yet those who have read in their entirety the correspondence of Adam Marsh, Robert Grosseteste and John Pecham, or who have endeavoured to pierce through to the personal experience and intimate characteristics of Albert the Great, Thomas Aquinas or Robert Kilwardby— to say nothing of the enigmatic Roger Bacon or Duns Scotus—will readily admit that in all the arts of language, in

[2] Héloïse is known as a writer only through her letters to her lover and husband, Peter Abelard, which reveal more of the writer's personality than is usual in medieval letters.—Ed.

[3] Peter Damian (1007–1072) attacked dialectic and reason in order to uphold the absolute supremacy of faith. He recommended that all intellectual activity should be restricted to the study of the Bible and its commentaries. John of Fécamp wrote prayers that were incorporated into the Roman missal, where they are attributed to St. Ambrose. William of Malmesbury (d. 1142) was the most literary and scholarly historian of his time.—Ed.

all manifestations of aesthetic feelings or personal emotions, in fine, in all the qualities of self-revealing intimacy, the great men of the thirteenth century are immeasurably poorer than their predecessors a hundred years before. And though the luminous and adequate expression of ideas and emotions does not of itself alone constitute a character which we call humanist—for neither Anselm nor Bernard, past masters of the craft of letters, are precisely humanists—yet the power of self-expression grounded upon, or at least reinforced by, a wide literary culture is a condition *sine qua non* of a humanist's growth.

The second trait of the humanism of the twelfth century was, it is suggested, a personal devotion to one or more of the great figures of the distant past. To look to the past as to an age wiser and more accomplished than the present, to imitate its masterpieces and hand on its doctrine, had been a common tendency in every country since the end of the Empire wherever any sort of enlightenment found scope. . . .

Abelard, Héloise and Ailred of Rievaulx[4] are among the comparatively few personalities of the early twelfth century whose lives and words will continue to attract and move the minds of men throughout the ages. All three are, though in very different ways, essentially of their own period and remote from ours in the circumstances of their lives and in the cast of their thought. The problems, the catastrophe and the fate of Abelard and Héloise are, quite as much as the austere monastic life of Ailred, typical of the twelfth century and remote from the experience of the twentieth. All three, on the other hand, by reason of their intense sensibility to emotions shared in some degree by all civilized mankind, and by reason also of a vivid power of self-expression, are not only of an age but for all time. With neither of the characteristics just mentioned are we concerned here, however, but with a third: the peculiar cast, that is, given to their thoughts and emotions by the humanistic training which they had undergone.

This appears, as has been said, most clearly in the reverence and devotion with which they regarded certain great figures of antiquity. With Abelard and Héloise it is Cicero, Seneca, Lucan and St. Jerome who are principally revered; with Ailred it is Cicero (at least in youth) and St. Augustine. That in the case of all three the influence has a strong religious colour and that its primary object is a saint (for St. Jerome is the exemplar to whom both Abelard and Héloise turn most readily) does not affect its peculiar character. . . .

The familiarity of all educated men of the age with the masterpieces of Latin literature has often been remarked upon. The mention of Héloise touches upon another aspect of this renaissance: the share, that is, of women in the higher culture of the day. Héloise, indeed, was something of a prodigy, but nowhere is there any suggestion that her uncle, Fulbert,[5] was acting in an eccentric or even in an unconventional manner when he decided to give his niece a perfect education in letters. Nor did she stand wholly alone. It may not be easy to point to individual *bas bleus*[6] in Paris or even in the convents of France in general, but in

---

[4] Ailred of Rievaulx (1110–1167) was a Cistercian abbot, spiritual writer, and historian. He grew up at the court of King David I of Scotland.—Ed.

[5] A canon of Notre Dame in Paris. He should not be confused with Fulbert of Chartres.—Ed.

[6] "Blue stockings," *i.e.*, educated women.—Ed.

England there was no lack of them. The daughter of Margaret of Scotland, the future Queen Maud, was given a thorough literary education at Wilton; Shaftesbury, a little later, sheltered Marie de France, and Muriel of Wilton was not the only other poetess in England,[7] as is shown by the numerous copies of Latin verses attached by the convents of women to the bead-rolls of exalted personages. These cloistered elegists, however, scarcely differ in kind from their sisters who, four hundred years before, had corresponded with St. Boniface; Héloise, alike in her single-minded enthusiasm, in her real literary powers, and in her devoted, even pedantic reverance for her classical models, is a true predecessor of Camilla Rucellai, Margaret Roper and Lady Jane Grey; to her, as to these, Dorothea in George Elliot's novel would have looked with admiration.

Héloise may well have outdistanced all rivals of her own sex. In deploring the lack of letters among men, however, Peter the Venerable, in his celebrated letter to the widowed abbess, is using the language of exaggeration, for no one acquainted with the literature of the age can be unaware of the wide familiarity shown by so many with Latin literature. Ailred of Rievaulx can assume a familiarity with Cicero's *de Amicitia* as a matter of course in a young Cistercian of his abbey; quotations from the poets are common in almost all the more elaborate chronicles and letters of the period; the greatest humanists, such as Hildebert of Chartres, Abelard and John of Salisbury, quote aptly and copiously from

a very wide range of Latin poetry. Rarely, perhaps, are the poets quoted solely on account of the intrinsic beauty of their words; Abelard, however, and John of Salisbury often give evidence of their appreciation of the purely poetic. For most the favourite authors are the rhetoricians and satirists of the Silver Age and the learned, artificial poets of the later Gallo-Roman culture. Though Virgil has pride of place, it may be suggested that even he may appear rhetorical to a superficial and unintuitive mind; Horace, significantly enough, is often quoted from the *Satires* and *Epistles*, rarely from the *Odes*—their beauty, it may be, was too sophisticated and too exquisite to be appreciated, their urbanity too unfamiliar, and their pagan morality and religion too obvious. For similar reasons Tibullus and Propertius rarely occur, and scarcity of manuscripts is sufficient of itself to account for unfamiliarity with Lucretius and Catullus. Juvenal, on the other hand, Lucan and the difficult Persius were, relatively speaking, more familiar to the contemporaries of Abelard than to classical scholars of to-day.

Nothing, perhaps, shows [more clearly] both the reality and the extent of the training on classical models than the facility with which numbers were able to compose sets of perfectly correct Latin verses, and that not only in hexameters and elegiacs, but in the lyric metres used by Horace and Catullus. That the inhabitants of nunneries in Wessex should have been able to write passable elegiacs, and that it should have seemed natural to a monk when composing a saint's life to break without warning or apparent reason into alcaics, hendecasyllabics and the still more elaborate iambic and trochaic metres, are phenomena of the late eleventh century to which it would be

---

[7] Marie de France (d. 1189), who told the stories of the Arthurian Romance in her *Lays*, probably became abbess of Shaftesbury. Muriel of Wilton was a nun of Wilton, who has been called "the earliest English poetess."—Ed.

hard to find a parallel save in the late fifteenth or early sixteenth. That only a few—a Peter Damian, an Abelard, a Hildebert—should have attained real poetry in their compositions should be no occasion for wonder; the rest fail where the most felicitous verses of a Jebb, of a Calverley, and even of a Milton fail; the remarkable fact is that so many had achieved a mastery of the language and the metre without any aid from a Gradus[8] or dictionary. Occasionally, indeed, the level of true poetry is attained, together with perfect felicity of vocabulary; Peter Damian's Sapphic hymns to St. Benedict, like the earlier hymn to the Baptist, *Ut queant laxis*, are supreme in their kind, and it would be difficult for a scholar, familiar only with ancient Latin literature, to assign their composition to the eleventh rather than to the sixth or the sixteenth century. More often, however, the nearest approach to true poetry is made in the simpler accentual metres and the lyrics that verge upon the vernacular.

The decline of this humanism, like its rise, was comparatively rapid. The phase of sentiment we are considering touched its apogee between the rise of Hildebert of Chartres and the central years of the literary life of John of Salisbury. With Peter of Blois the decline is beginning, and though in England there was something of a "time-lag," the end was reached with Walter Map, Gerald of Wales and their circle;[9] Gerald, indeed,

lived on into another world and lamented the change. By the death of King John the transformation was complete. The great figures of the early thirteenth century, whether thinkers or administrators, are all but inarticulate when not in their schools or chanceries. It is from the class of the unlettered, from a Francis of Assisi or a Joinville,[10] that the clearest utterances come, "the earliest pipe of half-awakened birds," heralding another dawn in Europe. Literary, philosophical, scholarly humanism was dead, and it is significant that the supreme and balanced art, the Pheidian assurance and repose of the sculptures of Chartres, of Wells, of Amiens and of Rheims, was the expression of life as seen, not by a Leonardo or a Michelangelo, but by unlettered handicraftsmen living wholly in the present and wholly ignorant of the literature and culture of the past.

This is not to say that the new age owed no debt, paid no homage, to the past. In one sense the debt of no century had been heavier; for, as recent scholarship has shown, a larger and larger portion of the corpus of Aristotelian writings and numerous dialogues of Plato and Greek philosophers of the Empire were becoming familiar to the West, together with works of science, Greek and Arabian. St. Thomas rests upon Aristotle, "the Philosopher," more completely and unreservedly than does Abelard upon Augustine or Jerome or Seneca; and, as regards language, all metal is tested upon the touchstone of Cicero. Plato, Aristotle and Augustine, in their various ways, are not merely the foundations of the fabric of scholasticism; they

[8] A dictionary showing the quantity of the syllables in Latin words.—Ed.

[9] Walter Map (*ca.* 1140–1209) held a position in the household of King Henry II of England. His *De Nugis Curialium* contains a lively picture of this court. Gerald of Wales (*ca.* 1146–1223) put his own personality into everything he wrote. His *Description of Wales* is perhaps his most valuable book, but his other writings are valuable (if not totally trustworthy) for his views on men and his times.—Ed.

[10] Jean de Joinville (d. 1317) accompanied Louis IX (St. Louis) of France on the Crusade, and in his old age wrote a life of the king in French notable for the bluff honesty with which he looked back on his experiences.—Ed.

are its *materia prima*, the very medium in which Aquinas works. Yet scholars of to-day who, when rightly demonstrating the traditional and wholly European character of medieval culture, emphasize the debt of the schoolmen to the ancients, may perhaps mislead those familiar only with modern history when they speak of the humanism, or of the classical tradition, of the great scholastics. The attitude of St. Thomas towards the masters of the past differs by a whole heaven from that of Abelard and Ailred, as it does from that of Erasmus and More. The humanists, though living in times so very different from those of Greece and Rome, scrutinize the lives and emotions of the ancients, imitate their modes of expression and seek to reach the heart of their thought by long and sympathetic examination; the schoolmen revere the past no less deeply, but it is the external, visible fabric of thought, the purely intellectual, impersonal element that they absorb, and so far from submitting themselves to its moulding influence, they adapt it without hesitation to serve a wholly new system of philosophy, an utterly different *weltanschauung*. To the schoolmen the personalities, the emotions, the external vicissitudes of the lives of Aristotle and Augustine meant nothing; the skeleton of their thought was all in all. To Ailred and to Héloise, as to the contemporaries of Cosimo de' Medici, the joy and anguish of an Augustine or a Cornelia were a consolation and a light; they turned to them, and to the poets of the past, for guidance and sympathy. "Then 'twas the Roman, now 'tis I." So the humanists, but never the schoolmen, found strength in a community of feeling with those who, centuries before, had trodden the same path, and it is this consciousness of the unchanging mind of man that divides the culture of the first Renaissance from the more familiar culture of the later Middle Age.

The subtitle of the journal *Patristique et Moyen Age*, referring to its contents as "studies of literary and doctrinal history," provides a summary of the professional interests of the editor, JOSEPH DE GHELLINCK, S.J. (1872–1950). This Belgian scholar was a professor at the Gregorian University and the Jesuit theological college at Louvain. His book on *The Theological Movement of the Twelfth Century*, published in 1914, established his reputation as an authority on the period. His later studies on medieval literature, especially the book from which the following passages are taken, added to this reputation. Having examined the conditions that produced a flourishing literature in the twelfth century, de Ghellinck concluded that scholastic methods and utilitarian interests overwhelmed the humanist tradition.*

Scholasticism as Destructive of the Humanist Tradition

The Latin literary culture, brought to such a height at the beginning of the century by Anselm and his contemporaries, Marbod, Baudri of Bourgueil, and Hildebert of Lavardin,[1] is carried on into the twelfth century by such refined and fastidious humanists as John of Salisbury, master of a humane wisdom

[1] St. Anselm (1033–1109) applied reason to further his understanding of matters of faith. Marbod of Rheims (1035–1123) wrote poetry and lives of saints. Baudri of Bourgueil (1046–1130) became archbishop of Dol and wrote poetry and a history of the First Crusade. Hildebert of Lavardin (*ca.* 1056–1133) was a poet noted for a classical Latin style and his interest in ancient Rome as shown in his description of Rome when he visited it.—Ed.

only to be found later in Petrarch (1304–1374), and by poets of note such as Adam of St. Victor [d. 1180] and Walter of Chatillon [*ca.* 1135–after 1189]. The sacred sciences were represented by writers who had received a good academic classical education and who knew how to write—writers like St. Bernard, a powerful orator, one of the best Latinists of his time; Hugh of St. Victor [d. 1141], of profound and clear intellect, in love with learning and contemplation, transparent in his style; Abelard, with a barbed pen, clarity of phrase and terseness of words, a lover of logic; Gerald of Wales [1147–1223], full of self-conceit,

* From Joseph de Ghellinck, *L'Essor de la littérature latine au XIIe siècle*, (Brussels and Paris: Librairie de l'Édition Universelle, S.A., 1946), vol. I, pp. 5–10, 14. Translated by Christine Hyatt. Footnotes omitted.

talkative, with a presumptuous style but an inexhaustible animation fed on caustic recollections. Sermons, most of them in Latin and consequently more learned and pedantic than popular, took on an importance in twelfth-century France and in the eyes of the writers attached to the Anglo-Norman courts, which has caused it to be said, not without exaggeration, that the French pulpit was never greater than at that time. History records a whole series of conscientious works which, without possessing the merits of the good Byzantine chroniclers, are well thought out and well written; beginning with the ingenuous Otto of Freising, at times an *enfant terrible,* and the reliable William of Malmesbury, the loyal William of Newburg,[2] who are followed by a line of historians who do honor to Anglo-Norman historiography. These writers, faithful to Latin exclusively for a long time, soon caused to recede into the background the editing of the Anglo-Saxon Chronicle, which had been going on, partially bilingually, since 915 at Winchester, Abingdon, Canterbury, and Peterborough; after 1140, in fact (the small addition of 1154 is of insignificant length), Latin was ultimately substituted for the work in old Anglo-Saxon inaugurated by Alfred the Great.[3] The stylistic demands become more evident the further one moves away from the dry manner of *Annals,* along with faithfulness to the rules of history, and unfeigned and honest criticism, following the model of Bede. The

epistolary genre offers copious selections of enjoyable readings often finely edited, valuable to anyone who wishes to penetrate the intimacy of those minds and those events: beside selections from the letters of Anselm, Hildebert, and Bernard, there are those by Geroch de Reichersberg, Hugh Metel, Ivo of Chartres, Suger of St. Denis, Guy de Bazoches and several crusaders, Peter the Venerable [abbot of Cluny, *ca.* 1122–1156], and several popes such as Innocent II, Alexander III, and Innocent III.

The other branches of learning too were cultivated. It was a flowering rarely seen so universally after a long period of barrenness. The remainder of the Middle Ages was not to experience such a vigorous literary development, or one so wholesome and so engaging: first there were attempts at moral and pastoral writing; preaching, more learned than popular, to judge by the evidence preserved; educational treatises which aspire to originality or are repetitive; ascetic writings and spiritual writings of an attractive freshness, an often discerning psychology, and a refined literary expression; canonical works, the latter the most prolific and fertile beginnings of the fine creative period of canon law. The qualities of some of these works give them a literary prominence. Others, more exclusively theological, such as biblical commentaries impoverished by ignorance of the original languages, and treatises on dogma connected with the *Liber Sententiarum,*[4] reveal a special technique which removes them from the field of literature but they remain instructive for the study of earlier methods

---

[2] Otto of Freising (d. 1158) wrote the *Book of Two Cities* and the *Deeds of the Emperor Frederick I.* William of Malmesbury (d. 1142) and William of Newburg (*ca.* 1136–*ca.* 1201) both wrote on English history.—Ed.

[3] Alfred the Great, king of Wessex from 871 to 899, is supposed to have originated the Anglo-Saxon Chronicle.—Ed.

[4] The *Sentences* compiled by Peter Lombard from the opinions of Church Fathers and other authorities became the standard textbook in theology in the medieval universities.—Ed.

of composition and the practice of theological style. The abundance of poetic writing includes works of lasting value, above all those in the rhythmical genre cultivated by Adam of St. Victor[5] and many others, with unusual taste and facility. But metrical verse was not forgotten. The twelfth century opens with the name of Hildebert of Lavardin and closes with that of Walter of Chatillon, true poets richly gifted, who cultivated both genres successfully, while Alan of Lille remained faithful to the classical rules.[6] Lyricism, satire (very much in fashion), and drama (rarer apart from religious drama and not very respectable), are the three areas where poetry was given a free rein.

All this literary production, from the time of the Carolingian reform, which had given the redeeming stroke, reflects the cultivation of ancient models: the old tradition of the Carolingian school which would have been even more enlightened had it not been abandoned after the twelfth century. It is seen in poetry and in prose, in the writings of theologians, philosophers, and ascetics, letter writers and preachers. This cultivation of ancient models is confirmed not only by the large number of classical quotations, the passing on of which was undoubtedly facilitated by grammatical instruction, but also by the persistence of rhetorical precepts down to the very details of expression, occasionally with a meticulous accuracy injurious to the spontaneity of the thought. Medieval Latin, eclectic by nature, as a result of selection from the models not strictly

classical, only rarely gives Cicero his true rank up to the time of Petrarch; but the language is, in general, correct and elegant, and usually free, except in the case of some exaggerated imitators of Valerius Maximus or Sidonius;[7] it has a delicacy of manner, a descriptive or satirical animation, always present, and often too a remarkable movement of vitality and life. Everywhere in these medieval Latin works the survival of the ancient and dependance on the classical past is apparent, even in the spiritual treatises on charity by the Cistercian Ailred,[8] who drew on the developments in the *De amicitia* of Cicero. It is revealed too in works in the vernacular, as the Anglo-Saxon translations written under the influence of Alfred the Great prove, and subsequently, in the *Disticha Catonis* to the Greek romance of Apollonius of Tyre,[9] translated just prior to the twelfth century through Latin intermediaries and from which the drama of *Pericles* derived in the time of Shakespeare. Evidence of the survival of these old Latin works, pagan and Christian, frequently anonymous, during medieval times is everywhere apparent. Traces of their influence are constantly being discovered in the relics of ancient Celtic, Anglo-Saxon, Romance, and Germanic literature: old apocrypha, legendary narra-

[7] The book of historical anecdotes written by Valerius Maximus (fl. A.D. 20) was used as a text in teaching rhetoric. Sidonius (*ca.* 431–*ca.* 482) was a Latin poet and letter writer.—Ed.

[8] Ailred of Rievaulx (1110–1167) was a spiritual writer and historian.—Ed.

[9] The author of the *Disticha Catonis* (Maxims of Cato) is unknown, but the work was attributed to the Elder Cato (the Censor) in medieval manuscripts. Composed in hexameters, this work was widely used to teach beginning students grammar, the art of poetry, and morals. Apollonius of Tyre is a Latin prose romance of the fourth or fifth century A.D. presumed to derive from a Greek original now lost.—Ed.

[5] Adam of St. Victor (d. 1180) was the author of the *Sequences*, which rank among the best religious poetry of the twelfth century.—Ed.

[6] Alan of Lille (*ca.* 1128–1202) wrote poems that may be described as philosophical-theological epics.—Ed.

tives of the Apostles and their contemporaries, allegories of the revised *Physiologus*,[10] descriptions of the *Mirabilia Mundi* [Marvels of the World] of the Pseudo-Aristotle, on the Orient, of the *Mirabilia urbis Romae* [Marvels of the City of Rome], the source of those of the twelfth century, the tales of the fabulists and oriental sayings, beside the more important works of the classical writers, prose writers, and poets, with which medieval thought is deeply impregnated.

This is not all; the activity of the twelfth century was directed outward, passionately, toward the philosophical and theological works of other peoples, Greek, Jewish, and Arab. This thirst for learning, stimulated too by the broad expanse of new horizons opened up by the Crusades and by relations with the Almoravids (1055) and the Almohades (1147) of the Caliphate of Cordova,[11] helped to paint the intellectual scene in the Europe of that time in extraordinarily warm, vivid, and glowing colours. There were translators at Seville and schools of translators at Toledo, which were visited by the English, the Dalmatians, the Italians; even Peter the Venerable sent a mission to Spain from Cluny, in Burgundy, to have the Koran translated; literati from Tuscany and Germany arrived at the court of Constantinople, drawn by the vain attempts at reconciliation of the Comneni,[12] and

the Normans, who had become masters of the Two Sicilys between 1061 and 1139, were eager to acquire learning through contact with Arab, Greek, and Byzantine works. Intense and varied, humanistic thought was revealed at that time as insatiable and tenacious, inventive in its initiatives, often audacious in its explorations, more than once free and independent in its conclusions. . . .

More than ever, and fortunately for our time, Romance and Germanic philology were joining forces with medieval Latin philology, in order to take more and more into account this fact: the two literatures, Latin and vernacular, cannot be studied in isolation or in watertight compartments; their works are explanatory the one of the other. The twelfth century saw the establishment of a genuine parallelism between the vigor of theology and the other academic disciplines faithful to Latin on the one hand, and the progress of works in national languages on the other, in spite of the preponderance of dialects. From a certain point in time the two went side by side. . . .

This Aristotelian encroachment, in the thirteenth century, brought about the origin of a method of teaching which broke with the old tradition of the Carolingian and Chartres schools, not only in the academic orientation and the choice of subjects, but also in the method of learning Latin, in the aims assigned to this apprenticeship, and in the utilitarianism that lowered the pitch of it. The classical *auctores* [authors] were abandoned for the benefit of grammatical and stylistic minutiae, without it being realized that for a language to be deprived of all communication with a living and spoken tongue meant losing at the same time all corrective against

[10] Written in the second century, this collection of marvelous animal stories was the source of much of the pseudobiology of later medieval writers.—Ed.

[11] The Almoravids were rulers of Northwest Africa and Moslem Spain until overthrown by the Almohades, a Berber confederation in Morocco. Contact with Arabic learning, and with Greek learning through the transmission by the Arabs, provided an important stimulus for the revival of learning in Western Europe.—Ed.

[12] Members of the family that ruled the Byzantine Empire from 1081 to 1185.—Ed.

spurious research and all support for maintaining a healthy continuity of life, elegance, and good taste. This change, which resulted in the decay of Latin, irremediably jeopardized the fate of medieval Latin literature. For, it must be admitted, from the first years of the thirteenth century its decline began to appear despite the brilliance of Latin culture in the twelfth century.

WILLIAM A. NITZE (1876–1957), a specialist in Old French literature, taught at the University of Chicago and the University of California at Los Angeles. Nearly all his books deal with Arthurian romance or are editions of manuscripts of the Grail romance. Unlike Haskins and several of the other authors quoted in the previous pages, Nitze maintains that the real spirit of the twelfth century is to be sought in the vernacular literature rather than the Latin literature of the period. His conclusions contrast the "revival" in the twelfth century with the rebirth that occurred in Italy in the fifteenth and sixteenth centuries. Although various modifications of Haskins' views have been suggested by later scholars, some of which are represented above, Nitze's article is one of the few direct statements completely opposing the whole concept of a twelfth-century renaissance to appear since the publication of Haskins' book.*

Contrasts Outweigh the Similarities

The frequent use of words or indeed names tends to wear down their meaning. They contract and at the same time expand their significance. We say "they are nice people," forgetting that the basic and long-prevailing meaning of "nice" was "ignorant" or "foolish" (NED). And so it is with the name "Renaissance," as commonly applied to the rebirth of antiquity in the fifteenth and sixteenth century—*Wiedergeburt des Altertums* [rebirth of antiquity], to use Burckhardt's classic phrase. I have always assumed that by rebirth Burckhardt meant, not a revival of something that was somnolent in the time, but actually

a new birth or re-creation of an ancient world that had been discovered anew. It is this idea that I should like to contrast with the Classical re-awakening of the twelfth century. The truth lies often in a shading, and in this instance the shading is of importance if we wish to keep our distinctions clear. . . .

This brings me to the nature of the contrast which to my way of thinking exists between the Rebirth of the fifteenth and sixteenth centuries and the Revival of the twelfth. The Middle Ages never knew that they were mediaeval. The men of the twelfth century had none of that awareness of a Cimmerian

* From William A. Nitze, "The So-Called Twelfth Century Renaissance," reprinted by permission from *Speculum*, XXIII (1948), published by The Mediaeval Academy of America, pp. 464–471. Footnotes omitted.

night from which—as Rabelais wrote his friend Tiraqueau in 1532—humanity had emerged. In reality they considered themselves "modern" in that to them Christianity was the coping-stone of the Roman arch and Antiquity a part (a substantial one, to be sure) of its structure. When Dante [1265–1321] referred (*Inferno*, IV, 131) to Aristotle as *"il Maestro di color che sanno"* [the master of the men who know] and to Vergil (II, 59) as the teacher whose *"fama ancor nel mondo dura,"* [fame still endures in the world] he was thinking in Christian, i.e., contemporary, terms. This is true not only of Aquinas, another of Dante's teachers, but also—to select a representative from the twelfth century—of the vernacular poet Chrétien de Troyes. In a noteworthy passage, which Gilson with characteristic insight has traced back to the Monk of St. Gall [late 9th century], Chrétien expressed himself as follows:

> Par les livres que nos avons
> Les feiz des anciiens savons
> Et del siecle qui fu jadis
> Ce nos ont nostre livre apris,
> Que Grece ot de chevalerie
> Le premier los et de clergie.
> Puis vint chevalerie a Rome
> Et de la clergie la some,
> Qui or est an France venue.
> Deus doint qu'ele i soit retenue
> Et que li leus li abelisse
> Tant que ja meis de France n'isse
> L'enors qui s'i est arestee.
> —*Cligés*, vss. 27–39

I translate or paraphrase as follows:

By the books which we have, the deeds of the ancients are known to us and the world as it formerly was. This our books have taught us, that Greece had the first fame of chivalry and of learning. Then chivalry came to Rome and the totality of learning now domiciled in France. God grant that it be kept there and that the place may please it to the end that never may the honor which is established there leave France.

Obviously, the twelfth century poet is proud of the cultural supremacy of his country. He glories in the fact that culture—that is, chivalry and learning—is domiciled in France. Once it had been the possession of Greece and Rome, so books tell us, but now it has journeyed west—as has the Greek youth of the story he is narrating, the *Cligés*, who (ironically) goes from Constantinople to the Arthurian court in Britain in order to learn manners or chivalry. I can discover in Chrétien's words no idea of a rebirth of Antiquity on French soil, a *humanitas* or *paideia* such as we associate with the Italian Renaissance. Chrétien is extolling no paganization of culture, no "attainment of self-conscious freedom" apart from theological considerations which the real Renaissance attempted. Of that Chrétien, like the rest of his contemporaries, knew nothing; and had he known, Augustinian that he was, he would have rejected it. So that, what the passage above shows is that the twelfth century was conscious of the continuity of Classical tradition, but hardly of a rebirth in the Renaissance sense and certainly not of a plan to make humanity over on an ancient model. . . . But the real spirit of the age—the *Zeitgeist*—is best seen in the vernacular authors whose concern was not only with ideas but also with the manners and customs of their contemporaries. . . .

So regarded, the twelfth century revival was complex and not confined to works of Latin or Classical inspiration. It included Celtic, Provençal, and even Arabic strains, to which Latin formed, so-to-say, the motivating background. And its expression was centered in the ducal or regal courts of Europe, of which the English or Angevin court, under Henry I and Henry II, was the leading example. When, in 1136, Geoffrey of Monmouth wrote his *Historia regum Britanniae*—the fountain-head of Arthurian romance and of English dynastic tradition—he cited a "certain very old book in the British tongue" as his source, although he was giving the Norman kings a Trojan descent and setting up King Arthur as a counterpart to Charlemagne. In similar fashion the *Roman de Thebes* of about 1155, though materially derived from Statius, mentions *fées* [fiefs] and celebrates chivalry (and learning) as if it had been an ancient or Greek institution. We all know what Benoit de Sainte More did with the story of Troy, which he derived not from Homer but from late Latin versions taken from Dares and Dictys and elaborated in typical mediaeval manner, so that the characters are not only courtly *à la* twelfth century but also one of them, Troilus, is barely known to Homer, and his love-affair with Briseïda (later Cressida), becomes a priceless mediaeval invention—the inspiration of Boccaccio, Chaucer, and Shakespeare. Says Chaucer:

In which ye may the double sorwes here,
Of Troylus, in loving of Criseyde,
And how that she forsook him or she dyde.

Not that Chaucer does not censure morally what he has set forth so poignantly. . . .

Chrétien de Troyes fitted admirably into this romantic, one might almost say baroque, atmosphere. His Classical baggage was not impressive. He drew principally on Ovid, less on Vergil, and hardly at all on Horace. For the simple reason that Ovid through the *Amores, Ars Amatoria,* and *Remedia Amoris* was the exponent and doctor of the "ruling passion." Had not Ovid observed,

"we praise old times but use the present age"? In this regard the twelfth century and particularly Chrétien were to support his view. The first four of Chrétien's Arthurian romances are love-stories; and two of them, the *Erec* and the *Ivain,* deal with the problem of "sloth," one of the seven deadly sins in mediaeval ideology. The *Historia regum Britanniae* had warned the Norman conquerors of this danger that peace and luxury engender. In Chrétien's romance, Erec's fault is that his devotion to Enide makes him slothful—in the words of Tennyson (who retold the story):

As of a prince whose manhood
was all gone,
And molten down in mere
uxoriousness;

and even the active Ivain, prodded by Gauvain, barely escapes the peril. The French poet discovered the theme in his Celtic source, where—to cite one specific example—it occurred in the old Irish *Serglige ConCulainn* or "Sick-Bed of Cuchulinn" in the form:

Shame on you to fall sick for the
love of a woman.

But he also remembered his Vergil and doubtless his Ovid, and the remedy that these poets had prescribed for lovers so afflicted. . . .

Obviously, the subject I have brought to your attention is not as simple as I here suggest. It could bear further research and elaboration. I have said nothing about Provençal and Arabic, both contributing factors to Angevin culture. I need not remind you that Adelard of Bath, who lived under Henry I, was the pioneer student of Arabic science and philosophy, and "the greatest name in English science before Grossetete [1175–1253] and Roger Bacon [*ca.* 1210–*ca.*

1292]." As for Provence, Chrétien knew Montpellier as a medical center as early as 1170 (*Lancelot*, vs. 3501), and himself drew on Bernart de Ventadorn, a Provençal, in his poetry. Nor should we forget the array of French Byzantine romances, beginning with the *Eracle* (Heraclius) of Gautier d'Arras, a contemporary of Chrétien; nor the so-called *Bible* by Guiot de Provins, who at the turn of the century flayed the nobility for their neglect of courtly manners.

But despite these and other omissions, I trust my main point is secure. For, whether civilization in the twelfth century began primarily with Latin, Celtic, or Provençal, or rather with the impact of these cultures on each other, the fact remains that the Classical element in it was chiefly background or coloring given themes that were indigenous in the practical life of the age and not freshly imported from the Ancients. If a comparison with a typical Renaissance theme were necessary to enforce my contention, I should choose Racine's masterpiece, *Phèdre*. Here we have, not a revival, but an actual "rebirth" of Euripides' *Hippolytos* and the *Phaedra* of Seneca....

These are some of the reasons why, as a mediaevalist, I prefer to render unto Caesar the things that are Caesar's and to leave the term *Renaissance* to the Renaissance. I agree with the late Louis John Paetow when he defined the period

we have been discussing as "civilization in Europe beginning with the close of the eleventh century" and added: "unfortunately this movement is now quite generally called 'the twelfth century renaissance.'" Certainly the Middle Ages and the Renaissance are not mutually exclusive, nor is the separation between them as marked in all European countries. We are bound to find more and more elements of one in the other, either as anticipations or as survivals: the stream of history is continuous, and "learning is a seamless garment." History may be compared to a tapestry with many strands of diverse provenience interwoven. Burdach, Haskins, Gilson, Jaeger, have done their share in making this clear. But the emphasis each age placed falls on a different aspect of the historical picture: in the one, on the continuity of the Classics as a preparation for Christian, chivalric ideals; and, in the other, on a break with the immediate past and a return to a Utopian Classical world. In this larger sense, nothing is served by confusing the dominant trend of the one historical period with that of the other, or Anselm's *credo ut intelligam* [I believe in order to understand] would be synonymous with the *cogito ergo sum* [I am thinking, therefore I exist] of Descartes, despite the fact that the latter statement had mediaeval forbears.

The thesis that humanism had a continuous influence from the twelfth century through the Italian Renaissance was given its fullest expression by PAUL RENUCCI (b. 1915), a professor and director of the Institute of Italian Studies at the University of Paris. His writings include two books on Dante, one of which is *Dante, Disciple and Judge of the Greco-Latin World* (1954). Of particular interest is the way in which he blends the renaissance of the twelfth century, thirteenth-century scholasticism, and the Italian Renaissance, interpreting the shift from scholasticism as no more than a change in emphasis.*

The Italian Renaissance an Outgrowth of the Twelfth-Century Renaissance

In the second half of the eleventh century advance signs of a renewal of classical culture began to appear in Western Europe. These took the form here and there of "humanistic" acts of faith, stylistic imitations better executed than the earlier ones, a new curiosity about ancient art, and lastly some translations from Arabic and Greek.

If one were to take note of the geographical location where these signs appeared, it would be seen that they were particularly frequent in two very different regions of civilization, the area between the Rhine and the Loire on the one hand, and in southern Italy and Sicily on the other. While a new interest in works revered in ancient times and in the extant testimonies of the Latin world was being awakened in northern France and the Rhineland, Sicily and southern Italy were beginning to play the role of intermediary between the three Mediterranean worlds.[1]

One can already see the outlines of the two essential phenomena of the medieval Renaissance: the concentration of intellectual research between the Rhine and the Loire, and the return of Greek works to the West through the gateway of the south. But these two events were still isolated from each other;

[1] That is, between Byzantine, Arabic, and Latin culture.—Ed.

* From Paul Renucci, *L'Aventure de l'humanisme européen au Moyen-Age (IVe–XIVe siècle)* (Paris: Société d'Edition les Belles Lettres, 1953), pp. 54–55, 59, 61, 68–69, 99–100, 170–172. Translated by Christine Hyatt. Footnotes omitted. Permission to publish the translation given without charge by the author.

103

the intellectual revolution of the twelfth and thirteenth centuries was not to break out until two movements came in contact: that of the commentators and that of the translators. Without the accession into France of translations made at Palermo or Toledo, Parisian thought would probably have lacked food;[2] these translations, in return, might not have had such a wide influence without the work of the northern schools, where they were analyzed, expounded, and illuminated. The fact is that none of them exerted any influence before they had passed through the *rue du Fouarre*,[3] where they received, if one may so express it, their charge of efficacy. . . .

At Chartres, which was at that time the most flourishing center of learning in France, the taste for Platonic philosophy combined with the desire to fathom all the ancient philosophies and bring them into harmony, and all the ancients were the object of a deferential admiration as much for the elevation of their thought as for the perfection of their literary art. Through its disciples Chartres exercised a considerable influence on the beginnings of the Renaissance of the twelfth and thirteenth centuries. Its masters, serious illustrators of the intellectual Greco-Latin civilization, leaned toward the ancients only through love of eternal truth; what they were seeking was less a new source of attraction or pleasure than a forgotten uniformity of convincing answers to the great questions that obsessed and perplexed them. They were in this last aspect the most direct initiators of the

intellectual movement that led to Siger of Brabant,[4] St. Thomas Aquinas, and Dante. The care they took in collecting and propagating the works of antiquity, the contacts they maintained with all the different intellectual circles of the century are sufficient to show that they took their task for a sort of apostleship. . . .

Hildebert of Lavardin, the men of Chartres, Abelard, these are the representatives of what one could call the spontaneous humanism of the first half of the twelfth century. Not one of them, with the exception of Thierry of Chartres,[5] a mere nomenclator in the business, borrowed anything from the newly discovered text: they had very much the same material at their command as the Carolingian men of letters, but their spirit was quite different. They were at the same time innovators and traditionalists. They did not seem to realize the great work of discovery which was in the making, even coming into existence not far away from them. Yet it was this work which was to govern the intellectual life of the next hundred and fifty years. We must therefore assign a special place to the disciple of the masters of Chartres who was both a humanist like his masters and a remarkable student of texts, none other than Adelard of Bath. . . .[6]

Although the spread of the texts that had been discovered was rapid and universal, not all the humanists of the late twelfth century came equally under their

---

[2] Translations of Aristotle were made in Sicily and in Spain, where Latin scholars were in contact with Arabic scholars who served as intermediaries between Greek thought and the Latin culture of Western Europe.—Ed.

[3] A street in Paris where the faculty of arts was located in the twelfth century.—Ed.

[4] Siger of Brabant's (d. 1281) philosophy was influenced by the Moslem philosopher Averroës. Many of Siger's propositions were condemned by the Church in 1277.—Ed.

[5] Thierry of Chartres (d. *ca.* 1150) attempted to reconcile Greek philosophy and the Scriptures. His *Heptateuchon* is an encyclopedia of the seven liberal arts.—Ed.

[6] Adelard of Bath (d. 1150) translated Arabic science and wrote a popular book on that subject.—Ed.

influence; the Greek-Arabic contributions affected them more or less according to whether they tended toward logic and mathematics or ethics and oratory. The "spontaneous" humanism of which Hildebert, Bernard of Chartres, and Abelard were the forerunners ran alongside the flood created by the translations without merging with it as yet; nevertheless, logic tended to escape from the *trivium* in order to form a second *quadrivium* with geometry, astronomy, and soon afterward metaphysics, as the answer to a new conception of philosophy. This last, which was to turn more and more toward ontological problems, gradually dissociated itself from narrative and sentimental literature, from which it ceased to expect by way of interpretation what was not to be found in it. In return, the tales of the ancient poets and romancers, recognized at last for what they are, sustained an immense romantic production in the vernacular: antiquity came out of the schools and became, strictly speaking, popular. The multiplication of legends is evidence of the vogue it enjoyed. And even in the fine arts Greco-Roman models began to exert their influence.

Whatever reservations one may have about the good quality of certain inspirations, the movement may justly be termed the Renaissance of the twelfth century—or more accurately of its second half. . . .

Is it justifiable to keep repeating that the Middle Ages lacked faith in man? We would gladly say the opposite since it considered him capable of fathoming the whole of nature without the aid of God, and with God, the whole Truth. Between the thirteenth and sixteenth centuries the definition of human abilities underwent a change. Of the two propositions: the Renaissance is the Middle Ages plus man, and the Renaissance is the Middle Ages less God, Gilson estimates the second as having the greater veracity. For my part, I believe that neither God nor man was ever entirely absent from either of the two periods or the two kinds of thought; the power of man was understood in a different way. In the twelfth and thirteenth centuries the majority of minds based this power on reason but with the reservation, or rather the advantage, that at the furthest bounds of its exercise Revelation would come to take over reason and perfect human knowledge. In this view there remains nothing that cannot be known. Where the light of Aristotle dies that of the Scriptures begins. Owing to the sudden development of peripatetic (Aristotelian) illumination, an intervention was necessary to stir up the final drama: as the two lights were seen to fall on the same expanse, it was perceived that they were mingled together. . . . If this idea of knowledge in two stages was implicitly rejected by the modern Renaissance, it was because from the first the crisis of Averroism[7] had seriously injured it. It was also because the new humanism endeavored to exercise the light of its reason, which was both more intense and more composite than that of Aristotle, in the intimidating realm of Revelation. Here, the *medium* of knowledge, the Scriptures, become in its eyes an *object* of knowledge, that is,

[7] Latin Averroism refers to the philosophical influence of Averroës (1126–1178) upon such philosophers as Siger of Brabant. At the center of the controversy provoked by this influence was the doctrine of the "double truth," which held that what was true in philosophy was not true in theology. These views were condemned by the Church. The interpretation of Averroism has changed with recent studies, and the older views, which tended to oversimplify both Averroës' thought and his influence in Europe, should be treated with caution.—Ed.

of strictly rational investigation. The criticism of dogma by reason shattered the alliance of reason and dogma. . . .

In the thirteenth century Italy, more than any other country in Europe applied itself to the school of France. For this it need make no excuses, any more than we need to for having sought Italy's lessons in the sixteenth. A school bench is not a bad place. Philosophy, science, literature, courtesy, all crossed the Alps in massive waves. But this material fell on a people for whom knowledge of the absolute had never been their first concern and in whom Roman magnificence was bound to arouse more love than Greek profundity. The teachings of Thomas Aquinas realized their hour of victory. Dante is the living witness. But it was in his Averroist interpretation that the philosophy of Aristotle captivated the most adventurous minds in Italy, those who were seeking new ways in science, politics, and ethics. On the other hand, many religious souls, refusing to accept Revelation as not having come to pass, challenged a thinker who, despite St. Thomas, gave arms to impiety. Thomist teachings did not succeed in commanding the whole of Catholic thought: from Petrarch [d. 1374] to Marsilio Ficino [d. 1499] there were numerous believers who demanded of Platonism or simple mysticism purer ways of progressing toward God. Nevertheless, the feeble passion of the Italian genius for metaphysical questions was the cause of a notable development of Latin Averroism, which had taken up its abode at Padua; it not only embodied there several leading ideas which caused conceptions of very different origin and complexion to circulate among them. but in it its device of the double process of understanding was seen to be more esteemed than the doctrine itself. Without

the divorce which it proclaimed between sacred and profane science, its severity would more likely have set the Italians against it than captivated them. But could one fail to recognize that in detaching philosophy from dogma Averroism offered an additional opportunity of recovering possession of antiquity in its genuine spirit? Besides Revelation, it threw down a bridge between what had been profane and what was tending to become so.

Here again the play of national tendencies resulted in a discrimination between the disciplines. Reversing the movement of thought of the thirteenth century, Italy made literature and ethics the vanguard of its intellectual revolution. It was a moment of equilibrium in which Rome and Greece, Virgil and Aristotle were linked in the same gratitude and equal love: Dante figured there, and with an imposing gesture appeared, in a flash of lightning, to render it eternal. But, the lightning over, it was quickly perceived that Rome had thrust Athens into the background as truly as Rome was then politics, ethics, and eloquence, and Athens the science of the absolute. In place of doctrinal disputes stylistic disputes broke out. Paris had had the Aristotelian dispute: Italy was to have the Ciceronian one. And the discovery of various Greek authors in the fifteenth century was not to alter things much. It resulted in a renewal of material but not of thought. The Florentine Hellenism was to remain exterior, formal. Its development took on the force of Latin culture as it appeared after the return of the historians and the dramatists. The second Hellenization in depth of the Western consciousness occurred in the sixteenth century and in France rather than in Italy. . . .

Is it true that "the Italians approached

antiquity much less by the imitation of thought and art . . . than by a return to the passions and sentiments of the ancient spirit"? It was probably the Roman spirit that Gebhart[8] meant in writing these lines. If it is so, one can admit that Italian humanism was closer to Rome by instinct than ours. Its ambition was in any case to become Romanized. Apart from a few dilettantes for whom Greece gave forth a more delicate perfume, its promoters and its champions made the Republic of Cicero or the Empire of Augustus—with a preference for the Republic toward the end—into their second fatherland, indeed their only fatherland, for they united in their hearts the Italy of the past with that of their own time. The ancient inheritance found itself somewhat Italianized by this. The universalist science of the Middle Ages was replaced by a culture not exempt from nationalism. We know what name was to be bestowed at the beginning of the sixteenth century on the foreigners who had come to leave their traces on the peninsula: the barbarians . . .

It was not there that Dante, despite the universalism of his political faith, failed to foresee it. While remaining a good scholastic, did he not preach the surpassing of theory by the literary art? And if the ancient world in his eyes was that of reason reasoning, was it not also that of order and beauty? If he seeks final illumination only in God, does he not ask of Virgil a blazing exposition of the ethics of Christ and of Aristotle to guide the Emperor, master here on earth of the whole of humanity? Great was the ardor of his faith. But was the ardor of his political hope any less? He was proud of his metaphysical science:

is it less than the "fine style which honoured him"—and for having learned it from Virgil?

In whichever direction one looks, the work of Dante presents, linked or intermingled, the final fruits of a declining humanism and the first fruits of a humanism in flower. It is not strange, however, that one should be mistaken in it. Are these not in fact the offspring of the same seeds? The very air was in the act of changing. It cannot be sufficiently reiterated that the new humanism was born of the old, whose vitality had been weakened by two centuries of existence and unfavorable events. If one is anxious to cut through the course of the ages, it must be done about 1150. The intellectual revolution that unfolded in France from the middle of the twelfth century to the end of the thirteenth was as decisive as that which occurred in Italy from 1350 to 1500. The first paved the way for the second. There was, moreover, an Italian humanist, Flavio Biondo,[9] who fairly recognized a continuity that was wrongly disowned by too many of his contemporaries.

Dante, then, was neither the forerunner of a Renaissance still in Limbo, nor the last champion of a dying civilization. His place is at the turning point of an ancient current which changed direction in changing climate. It is none the less remarkable for that. The more so as he played in this new orientation the role that one has a right to expect from a man such as he. He was one of the first to grasp this great surge of European thought. And no other has approached it with greater command and majesty.

[8] Emile Gebhart, *Les Origines de la Renaissance en Italie*. Paris, 1870.—Ed.

[9] Flavio Biondo (1392–1463), humanist and historian, was not typical of the attitude of Italian Renaissance writers toward the Middle Ages.—Ed.

PAUL OSKAR KRISTELLER (b. 1905) is a professor of philosophy at Columbia University. The titles of two of his books—*Latin Manuscript Books before 1600* (1953) and *Studies in Renaissance Thought and Letters* (1956)—indicate the subjects to which he has contributed during a productive scholarly career. He was elected a Fellow of the Mediaeval Academy of America. In the following lecture, given at Brown University on December 15, 1944, Kristeller warns that any comparison of the twelfth-century renaissance with the Italian Renaissance involves a comparison of two cultural movements that were themselves not uniform but full of complexities. Although his lecture was addressed to the problem of understanding the Italian Renaissance, his comments might apply with equal validity to the differences that have divided scholars in their interpretation of the twelfth-century renaissance.*

A Call for Historical Pluralism

Ever since 1860, when Jacob Burckhardt first published his famous book on the civilization of the Renaissance in Italy, there has been a controversy among historians as to the meaning and significance of the Italian Renaissance. Almost every scholar who has taken part in the discussion felt it was his duty to advance a new and different theory. This variety of views was partly due to the emphasis given by individual scholars to different historical personalities or currents or to different aspects and developments of the Italian Renaissance. Yet the chief cause has been the consid-erable progress made during the last few decades in the field of medieval studies. The Middle Ages are no longer considered as a period of darkness, and consequently many scholars do not see the need for such new light and revival as the very name of the Renaissance would seem to suggest. Thus certain medievalists have questioned the very existence of the Renaissance and would like to banish the term entirely from the vocabulary of historians.

In the face of this powerful attack, Renaissance scholars have assumed a new line of defense. They have shown that

* From Paul Oskar Kristeller, "Humanism and Scholasticism in the Italian Renaissance" in his *Studies in Renaissance Thought and Letters*, (Rome: Edizioni di Storia e Letteratura, 1956), pp. 553, 554–556, 561–562, 565–566, 580, 582–583. Footnotes omitted.

the notion embodied in the term *Renaissance* was not an invention of enthusiastic historians of the last century, but was commonly expressed in the literature of the Renaissance itself. . . .

Without questioning the validity of this argument, I think that there are also some more objective reasons for defending the existence and the importance of the Renaissance. The concept of style as it has been so successfully applied by historians of art might be more widely applied in other fields of intellectual history and might thus enable us to recognize the significant changes brought about by the Renaissance, without obliging us to despise the Middle Ages or to minimize the debt of the Renaissance to medieval tradition.

Moreover, I should like to reexamine the relation between the Middle Ages and the Renaissance in the light of the following consideration. Scholars have become so accustomed to stress the universalism of the medieval church and of medieval culture and also to consider the Italian Renaissance as a European phenomenon, that they are apt to forget that profound regional differences existed even during the Middle Ages. The center of medieval civilization was undoubtedly France, and all other countries of Western Europe followed the leadership of that country, from Carolingian times down to the beginning of the fourteenth century. Italy certainly was no exception to that rule; but whereas the other countries, especially England, Germany, and the Low Countries, took an active part in the major cultural pursuits of the period and followed the same general development, Italy occupied a somewhat peculiar position. Prior to the thirteenth century, her active participation in many important aspects of medieval culture lagged far behind that of the other coun-tries. This may be observed in architecture and music, in the religious drama as well as in Latin and vernacular poetry in general, in scholastic philosophy and theology, and even, contrary to common opinion, in classical studies. On the other hand, Italy had a narrow but persistent tradition of her own which went back to ancient Roman times and which found its expression in certain branches of the study of the arts and of poetry, in lay education and in legal customs, and in the study of grammar and of rhetoric. Italy was more directly and more continually exposed to Byzantine influences than any other Western European country. Finally, after the eleventh century, Italy developed a new life of her own which found expression in her trade and economy, in the political institutions of her cities, in the study of civil and canon law and of medicine, and in the techniques of letter-writing and of secular eloquence. Influences from France became more powerful only with the thirteenth century, when their traces appeared in architecture and music, in Latin and vernacular poetry, in philosophy and theology, and in the field of classical studies. Many typical products of the Italian Renaissance may thus be understood as a result of belated medieval influences received from France, but grafted upon, and assimilated by, a more narrow, but stubborn and different native tradition. This may be said of Dante's *Divine Comedy*, of the religious drama which flourished in fifteenth century Florence, and of the chivalric poetry of Ariosto [1474–1533] and of Tasso [1544–1595].

A similar development may be noticed in the history of learning. The Italian Renaissance thus should be viewed not only in its contrast with the French Middle Ages, but also in its relation to the

Italian Middle Ages. The rich civilization of Renaissance Italy did not spring directly from the equally rich civilization of medieval France, but from the much more modest traditions of medieval Italy. It is only about the beginning of the fourteenth century that Italy witnessed a tremendous increase in all her cultural activities, and this enabled her, for a certain period, to wrest from France her cultural leadership in Western Europe. Consequently, there can be no doubt that there was an Italian Renaissance, that is, a cultural Renaissance of Italy, not so much in contrast with the Middle Ages in general or with the French Middle Ages, but very definitely in contrast with the Italian Middle Ages. It appears from a letter of Boccaccio [1313–1375] that this general development was well understood by some Italians of that period, and we should keep this development constantly in mind if we want to understand the history of learning during the Italian Renaissance. . . .

The humanistic movement did not originate in the field of philosophical or scientific studies, but it arose in that of grammatical and rhetorical studies. The humanists continued the medieval tradition in these fields, as represented, for example, by the *ars dictaminis* and the *ars arengandi*,[1] but they gave it a new direction toward classical standards and classical studies, possibly under the impact of influences received from France after the middle of the thirteenth century. This new development of the field was followed by an enormous growth,

both in the quantity and in the quality, of its teaching and its literary production. . . .

If we look for the medieval antecedents of these various types of humanistic literature, we are led back in many cases to the Italian grammarians and rhetoricians of the later Middle Ages. This is most obvious for the theoretical treatises on grammar and rhetoric. Less generally recognized, but almost equally obvious is the link between humanist epistolography and medieval *ars dictaminis*. The style of writing is different, to be sure, and the medieval term *dictamen* was no longer used during the Renaissance, yet the literary and political function of the letter was basically the same, and the ability to write a correct and elegant Latin letter was still a major aim of school instruction in the Renaissance as it had been in the Middle Ages.

The same link between humanists and medieval Italian rhetoricians which we notice in the field of epistolography may be found also in the field of oratory. Most historians of rhetoric give the impression that medieval rhetoric was exclusively concerned with letter-writing and preaching, represented by the *ars dictaminis* and the somewhat younger *ars praedicandi*, and that there was no secular eloquence in the Middle Ages. On the other hand, most historians of Renaissance humanism believe that the large output of humanist oratory, although of a somewhat dubious value, was an innovation of the Renaissance due to the effort of the humanists to revive ancient oratory and also to their vain fancy for speech-making. Only in recent years have a few scholars begun to realize that there was a considerable amount of secular eloquence in the Middle Ages, especially in Italy. I do not hesi-

[1] These handbooks on the "Art of Writing" and the "Art of Oratory" made them subjects of professional study, but the narrowly utilitarian purpose of preparing clerks for ecclesiastical and secular chanceries helped to destroy the study of literature in the tradition of Chartres. —Ed.

tate to conclude that the eloquence of the humanists was the continuation of the medieval *ars aregandi* just as their epistolography continued the tradition of the *ars dictaminis*. It is true, in taking up a type of literary production developed by their medieval predecessors, the humanists modified its style according to their own taste and classicist standards. Yet the practice of speech-making was no invention of the humanist, of course, since it is hardly absent from any human society, and since in medieval Italy it can be traced back at least to the eleventh century. . . .

Thus we may conclude that the humanism and the scholasticism of the Renaissance arose in medieval Italy about the same time, that is, about the end of the thirteenth century, and that they coexisted and developed all the way through and beyond the Renaissance period as different branches of learning. Their controversy, much less persistent and violent than usually represented, is merely a phase in the battle of the arts, not a struggle for existence. We may compare it to the debates of the arts in medieval literature, to the rivaling claims of medicine and of law at the universities, or to the claims advanced by Leonardo [da Vinci] in his *Paragone* for the superiority of painting over the other arts. Humanism certainly had a tendency to influence the other sciences and to expand at their expense, but all kinds of adjustments and combinations between humanism and scholasticism were possible and were successfully accomplished. It is only after the Renaissance, through the rise of modern science and modern philosophy, that Aristotelianism was gradually displaced, whereas humanism became gradually detached from its rhetorical background

and evolved into modern philology and history. . . .

Modern scholarship has been far too much influenced by all kinds of prejudices, against the use of Latin, against scholasticism, against the medieval church, and also by the unwarranted effort to read later developments, such as the German Reformation or French libertinism, or nineteenth-century liberalism or nationalism, back into the Renaissance. The only way to understand the Renaissance is a direct and, possibly, an objective study of the original sources. We have no real justification to take sides in the controversies of the Renaissance, and to play up humanism against scholasticism, or scholasticism against humanism, or modern science against both of them. Instead of trying to reduce everything to one or two issues, which is the privilege and curse of political controversy, we should try to develop a kind of historical pluralism. It is easy to praise everything in the past which happens to resemble certain favorite ideas of our own time, or to ridicule and minimize everything that disagrees with them. This method is neither fair nor helpful for an adequate understanding of the past. It is equally easy to indulge in a sort of worship of success, and to dismiss defeated and refuted ideas with a shrugging of the shoulders, but just as in political history, this method does justice neither to the vanquished nor to the victors. Instead of blaming each century for not having anticipated the achievements of the next, intellectual history must patiently register the errors of the past as well as its truths. Complete objectivity may be impossible to achieve, but it should remain the permanent aim and standard of the historian as well as of the philosopher and scientist.

Suggested Additional Readings

Most books about the history of medieval culture discuss the twelfth-century renaissance. However, not many writers are as explicit as Paul Vignaux, *Philosophy in the Middle Ages* (New York, 1959), who asserted that "The Middle Ages developed intellectually through the action of two renaissances—the Carolingian renaissance and the renaissance of the twelfth century." Frederick B. Artz in *The Mind of the Middle Ages* (3d ed.; New York, 1962) is less obvious in his treatment because he used a very broad chronological organization, but the book provides a good introduction and has a full bibliography. Gordon Leff, *Medieval Thought* (Harmondsworth, Eng., 1958) has a clear summary of intellectual trends in the twelfth century. The diligent reader will find a wealth of information scattered throughout Ernst Robert Curtius, *European Literature and the Latin Middle Ages* (New York, 1953). Further guidance may be found in Martin R. P. McGuire, *Introduction to Mediaeval Latin Studies: A Syllabus and Bibliographical Guide* (Washington, D.C., 1964). Obviously, no one book is comprehensive enough to include everything about a subject that cuts across so many academic disciplines including Latin literature, vernacular literatures, philosophy, theology, art and architecture, law, science, and history. However, the references in the following books will serve to guide the reader who may wish to follow one of the disciplines, as well as the reader who seeks a broader understanding of the twelfth-century renaissance and the historical interpretation of the period.

For an appreciation of how the concept of a twelfth-century renaissance was developed by scholars, the reader should begin with Jacob Burckhardt, *The Civilization of the Renaissance in Italy* (first published in 1860). Burckhardt interpreted Romanesque architecture in the North as a renaissance, and he saw the *Carmina Burana* poetry of the twelfth century as a sign of the new birth that was to come to full flower in fourteenth-century Italy. Twenty years earlier, Jean Jacques Ampère in his *Histoire littéraire de la France* (Paris, 1840) wrote of a cultural moment in France at the end of the eleventh century which he thought had all the characteristics of a true renaissance: an expanded knowledge of antiquity, great vigor in thought, and a new impulse in the arts.

For an early survey of the criticism directed against Burckhardt's views of the Italian Renaissance and its relation to the Middle Ages, see Walter Goetz, "Mittelalter und Renaissance," *Historische Zeitschrift*, 98 (1907), 30–54. Goetz also protested a Middle Ages full of so-called renaissances. Émile Gebhart, *Les Origines de la Renaissance en Italie* (Paris, 1879) tried to answer the question why the renaissance developed in fourteenth-century Italy rather than in twelfth-century France (where it seemed on the verge of doing so). The French achievement was also emphasized when Achille Luchaire in his volume *Les Premiers*

Capetians in Ernest Lavisse, *Histoire de France*, II, Pt. 2 (Paris, 1911) applied the title "The French Renaissance" to the later eleventh and early twelfth centuries. Earlier, Charles V. Langlois, "Les Universités du Moyen Age," *La Revue de Paris*, 3d year, I (February 15, 1896), 788–820, had used "the first renaissance" for the twelfth century.

A book that had an important influence upon the development of medieval studies was G. Robert, *Les Écoles et l'enseignement de la théologie pendant la première moitié du XIIᵉ siècle* (Paris, 1909), although it has now been replaced by the completely rewritten volume by Gerard Paré, Adrien Brunet, and Pierre Tremblay. The pioneering work on *The Universities of Europe in the Middle Ages* (London, 1895) by Hastings Rashdall included a second chapter on "Abelard and the Renaissance of the Twelfth Century." How the rise of universities contributed to overshadowing the revival of classical literature during the twelfth-century renaissance was investigated by Louis J. Paetow, *The Arts Course at Medieval Universities* (Urbana, Ill., 1910). He wrote a sympathetic review of Haskins, *The Renaissance of the Twelfth Century* in *Speculum*, III (1928), 122–124, although he had earlier deplored the use of the term in his edition of Henri d'Andeli, *The Battle of the Seven Arts* (Berkeley, Calif., 1914) and his *Guide to the Study of Medieval History* (Berkeley, Calif., 1917).

The theme of cultural continuity is found in Henry O. Taylor, "A Medieval Humanist: Some Letters of Hildebert of Lavardin," *Annual Report of the American Historical Association for the Year 1912*, pp. 89–94. In *The Mediaeval Mind* (London, 1911) he argued that "A part of the serious historian's task is to get rid of 'epochs' and 'renaissances'—Carolingian, Twelfth Century or Italian. For such there should be substituted a conception of historical continuity, with effect properly growing out of cause." Continuity was also emphasized by Edmond Faral, *Recherches sur les sources latines des contes et romans courtois du*

Moyen Age (Paris, 1913), who maintained that the romances of the twelfth century, although written in the vernacular, formed part of a literary tradition rooted in the distant Roman past. The part played by American historians in the development of the idea of the twelfth-century renaissance is discussed in Hans R. Guggisberg, *Das europäische Mittelalter im amerikanischen Geschichtsdenken des 19. und des frühen 20. Jahrhunderts* (Basel and Stuttgart, 1964).

The twelfth-century renaissance will always be particularly associated with the name of Charles Homer Haskins. In addition to his book *The Renaissance of the Twelfth Century*, now available in paperback, the reader should consult his *Studies in the History of Mediaeval Science* (Cambridge, Mass., 1924), *Studies in Mediaeval Culture* (London, 1929), and *The Rise of the Universities* (Ithaca, N.Y., 1957). A recent brief introduction to this renaissance can be found in Marshall Clagett *et al.*, *Twelfth Century Europe and the Foundations of Modern Society* (Madison, Wis., 1961). An excellent, somewhat longer account is David Knowles, *The Evolution of Medieval Thought* (Baltimore, 1962), which deals primarily with intellectual developments in the twelfth and thirteenth centuries. Richard W. Southern in an article on "The Place of England in the Twelfth-Century Renaissance," *History*, XLV (1960), 201–216, showed that the impulse for a renaissance came from the Continent, rather than from surviving remnants of Anglo-Saxon learning, and then developed certain characteristics peculiar to England.

The influence of classical antiquity upon the leaders of the twelfth-century renaissance has been explored by scholars in several disciplines. James Bruce Ross, "A Study of Twelfth-Century Interest in the Antiquities of Rome," in *Medieval and Historiographical Essays in Honor of James Westfall Thompson* (Chicago, 1938) found an interest and genuine historical understanding of the material remains of ancient Rome among some writers of the twelfth century. That there was a continuity of classical influence from Gallo-Roman art to Romanesque is the thesis of Jean Adhémar, *Influences antiques dans l'art du Moyen Age français* (London, 1939). On the other hand, Erwin Panofsky and Fritz Saxl, "Classical Mythology in Mediaeval Art," *Metropolitan Museum Studies*, IV (1932–33), 228–280, argued that while both classical form and classical subject matter were known, the two were not joined into a unified artistic whole by medieval artists. Eva Matthews Sanford, "The Study of Ancient History in the Middle Ages," *Journal of the History of Ideas*, V (1944), 21–42 reached similar conclusions in regard to the quite different subject she investigated, that is, medieval historians had a sense of continuity with the ancient past yet made critical use of classical historical materials. Another important article that examines the thought of the twelfth century in relation to antiquity is Hans Liebeschütz, "Das zwölfte Jahrhundert und die Antike," *Archiv für Kulturgeschichte*, 35 (1953), 247–271.

The variety of interests cultivated in the twelfth century make it difficult to represent all in a short list of titles. Helen Waddell, *The Wandering Scholars* (Boston and New York, 1927) is a justly famous book on the Latin poetry of the Goliards. How the ecclesiastical use of Latin, especially the approach to Biblical translation as the word of God, influenced the Latin language of the twelfth century is the theme of M. Hubert, "Quelques aspects du latin philosophique aux XIIᵉ et XIIIᵉ siècles," *Revue des études latines*, 27 (1949), 211–231. Vernacular literature was discussed in a general way by Urban T. Holmes, Jr., "The Idea of a Twelfth-Century Renaissance," *Speculum*, XXVI (1951), 643–651. A lengthy recent study of the same subject is Reto R. Bezzola, *Les Origines et la formation de la littérature courtoise en Occident* (3 vols.; Paris, 1958–63). The significance of the twelfth century is seen in his thesis that the form of European culture was fixed in that century, and that the combination of an ideal of the man of action and the man of thought produced the ideal of the cultivated gentleman

that dominated literature until the seventeenth century. Two specialized aspects of twelfth century studies, science and theology, are covered in R. P. Chenu, "Découverte de la nature et philosophie de l'homme à l'école de Chartres au XIIᵉ siècle," *Journal of World History*, II (1954), 313–325, and his *La Théologie au douzième siècle* (Paris, 1957).

Étienne Gilson in *Héloise and Abelard* (Chicago, 1951) pursued the theme of Christian humanism and emphasized that Héloise was a mixture of classical education and medieval Christianity. The concept is carried one step further by Martin R. P. McGuire, "Mediaeval Humanism," *The Catholic Historical Review*, XXXVIII (1953), 397–409, who concluded that the synthesis of learning by St. Thomas Aquinas in the thirteenth century was part of the current of Christian humanism and the basis for modern Christian humanism. Similar in treatment is Gerold G. Walsh, *Medieval Humanism* (New York, 1942). Douglas Bush, *The Renaissance and English Humanism* (Toronto, 1939) argued that Christian humanism as exemplified by John of Salisbury was perpetuated in the later Renaissance. A curious reversal of emphasis is Jacques Boulenger, "Le Vrai siècle de la Renaissance," *Humanisme et Renaissance*, I (1934), 9–30, who found the true century of the renaissance in twelfth-century France, rather than the later derivative movement in Italy.

The relation of medieval renaissances to the Italian Renaissance is implicit even in the terminology, and this question has been the subject of much debate. The most radical book is John Nordström, *Moyen Age et Renaissance* (Paris, 1933), who used the twelfth century to attack the views of Jacob Burckhardt. Geoffrey Barraclough, "Medium Aevum: Some Reflections on Mediaeval History and on the Term 'The Middle Ages,'" in *History in a Changing World* (Oxford, Eng., 1957), pp. 54–63, looked at the influence of renaissance conceptions in forming the idea of a Middle Ages. One of the most perceptive examinations of the intellectual movement in the twelfth century and its special characteristics that contrast with the Italian Renaissance is Erwin Panofsky, "Renaissance and Renascences," *The Kenyon Review*, 6 (1944), 201–236. He later expanded these ideas in a book entitled *Renaissance and Renascences in Western Art* (Stockholm, 1960). Two booklets that provide excellent introductions to the problem of the Italian Renaissance are:

Denys Hay, *The Renaissance Debate* (New York, 1965) and William J. Bouwsma, *The Interpretation of Renaissance Humanism* (2d ed.; Washington, D.C., 1966). The best and most comprehensive book on the historiography of the renaissance problem, including some information on the idea of a twelfth-century renaissance, is Wallace K. Ferguson, *The Renaissance in Historical Thought* (Boston, 1948).